VIRGINIA'S PRESIDENTS

A HISTORY & GUIDE

HEATHER S. COLE

THE
History
PRESS

Published by The History Press
Charleston, SC
www.historypress.com

First published 2023

Manufactured in the United States

ISBN 9781467152686

Library of Congress Control Number: 2022947082

Dedicated to my two favorite young historians, Nick and Aiden.

The author's children at Yorktown Battlefield. *Author's photograph.*

CONTENTS

PREFACE

WHY ANOTHER BOOK ABOUT U.S. PRESIDENTS?

There are literally hundreds of books written about the presidents of the United States, and it is not my goal to duplicate the efforts of historians who have spent decades examining every detail of their lives. Instead, I hope that this book will be of interest to the casual reader who would like to learn a bit more about the eight U.S. presidents who were born in Virginia and the historic homes and sites mentioned within. Hopefully, this book will provide the background information necessary to make readers more-educated visitors and inspire questions for the tour guides and museum staff they may encounter in their travels. Each chapter also includes details on the various museums, historic sites and presidential homes in Virginia and nearby areas.

The origin of this book was a project I undertook with my elementary school–aged children several years ago. At the time, I was homeschooling them and was looking for a way to keep everyone's brains engaged over the summer break. I stumbled across the factoid that more United States presidents were born in Virginia than in any other state, and I decided that we would spend the summer visiting their homes. My two boys were still young enough to tolerate such an adventure, bribed by promises of visits to the museum gift shops afterward. (For anyone contemplating such a project with the young people in their lives, I've included a list of recommended children's books in the bibliography.)

The author's son posing with reenactors at George Washington's Mount Vernon. *Author's photograph*.

In 2021, I started working as a part-time tour guide for the Woodrow Wilson Presidential Library and Museum in Staunton, Virginia. In addition to the school and senior groups, there were a fair number of visitors who were doing some version of what my kids and I had done: visiting all the presidential libraries, all the historic sites related to Woodrow Wilson or all the homes of all our presidents (an ambitious undertaking). In providing recommendations to visitors about where to travel next, I discovered that there was no guide to the homes of Virginia presidents that was still in print. I hope this book will fill that niche.

CHANGING INTERPRETATION OF HISTORIC SITES

If you haven't visited a historical museum in a few years—or if the last time you read about our presidents was in high school—you may be a bit surprised by how the historical interpretation of our presidents has changed. Most presidential homes and museums no longer uncritically celebrate the lives of our presidents. Instead, they acknowledge what previous generations either ignored or downplayed: the fact that every one of the U.S. presidents born in Virginia was born into a home that was supported by the labor of enslaved people. Enslaved women cooked for them, cleaned up after them and may have served as wet nurses for them when they were infants. Enslaved children were their playmates and personal servants. As adults, seven of the eight Virginia presidents bought, sold and inherited enslaved people, who labored in their homes, fields and factories. This unpaid labor produced tobacco and commercial goods that were sold in order to build up the wealth of their owners. Without the wealth generated by enslaved labor, none of the first seven Virginia-born presidents could have lasted long in the political world, where the expenses of serving in Congress, the statehouse or the White House were greater than the salary they earned. In several cases, our future presidents sold enslaved workers in order to pay debts accumulated during their political careers. At least one Virginia-born president—and possibly four others—fathered children with women whom they enslaved.

Why does this matter? Well, what we learn about the past influences how we understand our place in the present. We need to understand that our founding fathers—and those who came after—were brilliant, talented and flawed people who created and upheld a brand-new form of government that has served us well for nearly 250 years *and* was built on the belief that the "all men...[who are] created equal" only included white, landowning men and that "We, the people, of the United States" explicitly excluded people of color, Native Americans and women. All Virginia presidents—from George Washington to Woodrow Wilson—supported some variation of these beliefs and used their power to, among other things, force indigenous people off their land, perpetuate the institution of slavery in new states and territories and prevent women from obtaining the right to vote. Lest we annul these offenses by claiming that the Virginia presidents were merely products of their eras, it is important to know that, at the same time, there were other leaders in other parts of the United States who were fighting for the abolition of slavery, a stop of westward expansion and equality for women.

Presidential sites are not the only places where these changes in historical interpretation have occurred, but they are some of the most visible due to their popularity. And many of the sites mentioned in this book have been working on their interpretations for decades. Take, for example, Thomas Jefferson's Monticello. When the Thomas Jefferson Memorial Foundation purchased the house in 1923, its stated goal included that the house "be forever retained as a shrine," implying a fairly uncritical view of Jefferson's life. By 2000, the foundation had accepted the DNA evidence that Jefferson had fathered the children of Sally Hemings, a woman whom Jefferson had enslaved, and today, Hemings's story is a central part of the site's interpretation. James Monroe's Highland and John Tyler's Sherwood Forest both have independent researchers tracking down information on the enslaved people who lived at the plantations. George Washington's Mount Vernon, James Madison's Montpelier and Woodrow Wilson's birthplace already include information about the enslaved in their exhibits and tours.

New Tools to Study History

When contemplating how we know what we know about the past, it is also important to remember that history is not static but an ever-changing and dynamic field. The stories we tell about our past evolve over time, as historians discover new sources and ask new questions. For generations, classical history focused on the stories of "great men" and "great events" (usually kings and wars). In the early part of the twentieth century, historians first started to become interested in class conflict and used that as a lens through which to interpret events of the past. The civil rights movements of the 1960s and 1970s influenced historians to begin telling the stories of women, immigrants and Native Americans, whose lives were illuminated through journals, letters and oral histories. New technology in the 1980s and 1990s allowed historians to analyze vast amounts of data

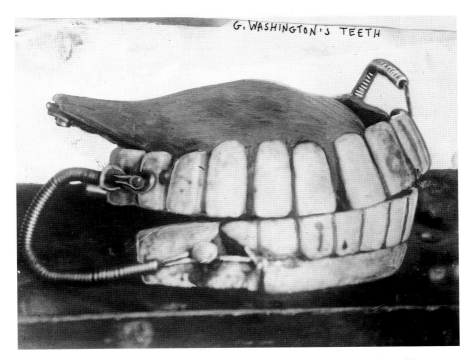

George Washington's teeth, currently on exhibit at George Washington's Mount Vernon. *Library of Congress, Prints and Photographs Division.*

from census and other records for the first time, allowing for economic and demographic interpretations that would have previously been impossible. And today, we have tools like DNA that can tell us stories that are completely missing from the written record. Over time—sometimes too much time—these new historical interpretations make their way into our schools, museums and popular culture.

This process has not been easy, and not everyone accepts the new historical interpretations. As a tour guide at Woodrow Wilson's birthplace, I received pushback from the occasional visitor who thought we were unfairly applying twenty-first-century standards to nineteenth-century individuals. And as I write this in the spring of 2022, the board of directors of James Madison's Montpelier—previously celebrated for its inclusion of the descendants of people enslaved at Montpelier in its interpretation—is now embroiled in controversy over how to involve descendants in the future management of the property.

I happen to think that these controversies are good. I love to see people and organizations grappling with the past and trying to figure out what relevancy it has in the present. To quote Spanish philosopher George Santayana, "Those who cannot remember the past are condemned to repeat it." However, it's not just about remembering; we must also discover, interpret and share—and always be open to looking at things in a new way.

I am reminded of my favorite memory from our summer of presidential homes: my kids and I took the family-friendly tour of Madison's home, "Discovering Montpelier." The tour focused on the process of historical discovery, and in each room, the tour guide shared an artifact from Madison's life (a letter, a painting, a scrap of wallpaper, et cetera) and talked about how it was discovered and how it shed light on something about him, his family or the house. The guide ended the tour by reminding us that historians continue to make discoveries about the house and sent us to their archaeology lab to see how newly discovered artifacts are cleaned, labeled and stored. My ten-year-old was absolutely enthralled by that idea that he, too, could make an important historical or archaeological discovery. When he found a bit of discarded scrap metal half-buried near the Montpelier parking lot, he dug it out and insisted that we take it to the museum staff. He spent the next few weeks constantly on the prowl for more "artifacts."

It is just that curiosity and enthusiasm that I hope every reader brings to their own historical exploration, whether it be in their living rooms, backyards or across Virginia and beyond.

ACKNOWLEDGEMENTS

T hank you to my editor Kate Jenkins and the staff at The History Press for their support of this book. Thanks to the editors of the *VA Voice*, where I initially published an article about our presidential homeschooling adventures. Thanks also to all the staff and volunteers at organizations across Virginia and Washington, D.C., who gave tours, answered questions and tracked down images for this book; they include: Daniel Addison, Anette Ahrens, Dustin Baker, Matt Briney, Shelby Chandler, Michael Cohen, Amy Cotz, Camille Dierksheide, Annique Dunning, Rachel Eavey, Hunter Hanger, Elizabeth Karcher, Jarod Kearney, Marianne Martin, Mary Massie, John McKee, Donald Moro, Lori Pikkaart, Cynthia Polhill, Tammy Radcliff, Farron Smith, Jeni Spencer, Bethany Sullivan and Frances Tyler. Finally, thank you to my proofreaders, Josh Cole, Lorrie Duewiger and Barbara O'Connor. Any remaining mistakes are my own.

1

GEORGE WASHINGTON

Our First President

FAST FACTS ABOUT GEORGE WASHINGTON

- First president of the United States.
- Born February 22, 1732; died December 14, 1799.
- Served two terms: 1789–97.
- Married Martha Dandridge Custis (1731–1802) in 1759.
- Stepchildren: John Parke Custis (1754–1781) and Martha Parke Custis (1756–1773).
- Nicknamed "His Excellency" and "Father of His Country."
- Only president who was unanimously elected.
- Only president who never lived in the White House.
- Prior careers: surveyor, military officer and planter.

ALL ABOUT GEORGE WASHINGTON

So much that we think we know about our first president is wrong. He did not chop down a cherry tree and then tell his father that he could not tell a lie. He did not throw a coin across the Potomac River. He never wore wooden teeth. (But he did wear dentures that were made, in part, from teeth extracted from enslaved people.) The mythology that swirls around George

George Washington, the first president of the United States. *Library of Congress, Prints and Photographs Division.*

Washington speaks to the heroic status he has in American history—a status that was present during his lifetime as well. The stories that we tell about Washington speak to the qualities we expect in a hero: honesty, strength and endurance. How well did Washington meet those expectations both during his lifetime and today, as we look back on his legacy?

Early Life

The first president of the United States came from more modest roots than the Virginia-born presidents who came after him. George Washington's maternal grandmother was an indentured servant who left her daughter—Mary Ball—an orphan at the age of twelve. Washington's father, Augustine, was one of the poorer members of Virginia's ruling class. When the two married in 1731, Augustine was a widower with two young sons and was fourteen years older than Mary. The family moved to a plantation in Westmoreland County, Virginia, called Popes Creek. It was here, on February 22, 1732, that the couple's first son, George, was born.

When George was six years old, the Washington family moved to a plantation located across the Rappahannock River from Fredericksburg, Virginia. They called it Home Farm, and today, it is called Ferry Farm. Mary had five additional children there, including one who died in infancy.

In 1743, Augustine died, and his estate was divided among his heirs. George inherited the Home Farm; the oldest Washington son, Lawrence, inherited the property on the Potomac River that would eventually be known as Mount Vernon. After Augustine's death, Mary struggled to make the Home Farm plantation support her family and the twenty enslaved staff who lived and worked there. Although his older half-brothers had been educated abroad, there was no extra money for George or his younger siblings to go away to school. At the age of seventeen, George went to work.

George Washington had initially imagined a life at sea for himself, but his mother strongly objected. Instead, his half-brother Lawrence stepped in and used his contacts to help George get his first job. Lawrence had married into a wealthy Virginia family who owned undeveloped land in the mountains of western Virginia, and George was given the job of surveying the lands. That experience got George first dibs on purchasing land for himself, which he would later resell at a profit.

Lawrence also facilitated his brother's first and only trip to a foreign country. In 1751, he asked George to accompany him on an extended trip to Barbados in the hopes that the climate would help his recovery from tuberculosis. It failed, and Lawrence died the following year. During the trip, George caught smallpox but recovered, and the immunity he gained protected him later in life.

Lawrence's death was undoubtedly difficult for the Washington family, but he left two final gifts for his younger brother: in his will, Lawrence directed

George Washington's Ferry Farm, a modern reconstruction of Washington's boyhood home. *Photograph by EagleOne Photography and courtesy of George Washington's Ferry Farm.*

that George should inherit the Mount Vernon plantation if he outlived Lawrence's wife and daughter (which he did). Lawrence's death also left a job opening in the Virginia militia, which George worked his brother's connections to obtain for himself.

Washington Starts a War

While George Washington is best known for leading colonial troops in the American Revolution, he cut his teeth during the French and Indian War (1754–1763), a war that he may have inadvertently started. From around 1600 to 1750, France claimed the bulk of North America west of the Appalachian Mountains but had little control over the area due to a lack of settlers. The French did, however, want to protect their claim from the British, who were beginning to expand west of the mountains.

In 1754, a twenty-two-year-old Lieutenant Colonel George Washington and his troops were sent by the governor of Virginia into the upper Ohio River

Valley to shore up British-claimed territory. Along the way, Washington and his Iroquois (Mingo) allies encountered a group of French Canadians, then ambushed and killed them. The group included a French diplomat, and his killing was a violation of international protocol, for which Washington was blamed. The French retaliated a month later with an attack on Washington's troops at Fort Necessity, Pennsylvania. And the war was on: the French and their Native American allies versus the British, British colonists and their Native American allies.

The following year, Washington redeemed himself while serving under General Edward Braddock on an ill-fated trip back into the Ohio River Valley. Braddock was killed, along with two-thirds of the British troops. Washington rallied the survivors and led them in a retreat under heavy French fire. His superiors recognized Washington's leadership skills, and he was given command of the defense of the western frontier of Virginia. From 1754 to 1758, Washington led several military expeditions west of the Appalachian Mountains, learning how to travel and fight in rugged terrain— skills that would serve him well in the future—and gained a reputation as a valiant leader, even while losing more battles than he won.

When the French and Indian War finally ended in 1763, France relinquished all land east of the Mississippi River and much of what would eventually become Canada to Great Britain. France also relinquished to Spain the land south and west of the Mississippi, effectively ending French colonial presence in North America. Washington was championed as a war hero.

Family Life at Mount Vernon

While on leave, George Washington took a trip back east to Williamsburg, Virginia, to meet the woman who would change the course of his life and his fortune: Martha Dandridge Custis. Martha was a twenty-seven-year-old widow with 2 children, 290 enslaved people and eighteen thousand acres of land, making her one of the wealthiest women in the colony of Virginia. George began courting Martha in 1758. By then, he was renting Mount Vernon from Lawrence's widow, and he had added a second story onto the house in anticipation of his upcoming nuptials. Washington resigned from the military in December 1758, and the couple married on January 6, 1759. Martha and her children, Patsy (age two) and Jack (age four), moved into Mount Vernon, and the family of four started their new life together.

Washington's Return to Mount Vernon on Christmas Eve, 1783. Print from a painting by Jennie Brownscombe. *Library of Congress, Prints and Photographs Division.*

Throughout his military service during the American Revolution and two terms as president, Washington spoke and wrote of his longing to return to his home along the Potomac River in Virginia, Mount Vernon. It was likely the memories of those first years as a small family that he cherished. Martha likely spent her days supervising the enslaved and indentured house staff and seeing to her children's education. Washington set about expanding his land holdings and experimenting with new farming techniques. By 1775, he had doubled the size of the plantation and the population of enslaved workers who lived and worked there.

In addition to Mount Vernon and the Home Farm (where his mother lived until 1772), Washington also managed the eighteen-thousand-acre tobacco plantation that belonged to the estate of Martha's late husband. During this time, Washington also traveled regularly to Richmond, where he served in the Virginia House of Burgesses, the legislative branch of the colony. It was this last role that would draw him away from his beloved Mount Vernon for most of the next two decades.

The American Revolution

The French and Indian War was the western theater for a much larger Seven Years' War (1756–1763), that was largely fought between Great Britain and France over control of territory in North America, India and the Caribbean. The war left Great Britain close to bankruptcy, and the nation saw the American colonies as a source to pay their war debts, largely through taxation. The colonists, however, were agitating for greater self-government and felt they were being treated as second-class citizens by the British government. As the population of the colonies grew, more people sought to move west of the Appalachian Mountains, to land that King George III had proclaimed was closed to settlement. Colonists responded to what they believed were unfair restrictions by attempting a boycott of British goods and, in Massachusetts, the infamous Boston Tea Party (December 1773).

A group of representatives from twelve of the thirteen colonies met in the fall of 1774 to articulate their grievances to Great Britain and discuss the formation of a local unified government. The meeting would come to be known as the First Continental Congress. The colonists' complaints were largely ignored by the king. By the time the Second Continental Congress met the following spring, war had already broken out in Massachusetts (the April 1775 Battles of Lexington and Concord).

Over the next several months, delegates worked to form a provisional government (in the form of the Articles of Confederation) and gain the support of their home colonies. They also voted to raise an army and asked Washington, one of the delegates from Virginia, to serve as commander in chief. The American Revolution had begun.

George Washington spent almost the entire eight years of the American Revolutionary War in the field with his soldiers. By his side was his enslaved manservant Billy Lee. After some troubling losses early on, Washington adopted a "hit and run" military strategy that involved surprise attacks followed by retreats. Washington knew that he was outnumbered and out-trained by the British troops but hoped that the British would eventually run out of stamina and withdraw.

Unlike the British, who had a professionally trained army, Washington had to make do with a largely volunteer military whose members served only yearlong enlistments. He had trouble recruiting soldiers, so he permitted freed Black men to fight, making the American Revolution the only major American conflict fought with integrated troops until the Korean War. Congress also struggled to get states to raise funds for the military, which meant that Washington's troops were often underfed and poorly clothed. They also suffered through several smallpox outbreaks, which Washington, due to his earlier exposure in Barbados, survived unscathed. The army's darkest time was likely the winter of 1777–78, when an estimated 1,700 men died in the Continental Army's encampment in Valley Forge, Pennsylvania.

By the following spring, Congress had passed legislation that said soldiers would be paid if they signed on for the duration of the war. At last, Washington was able to fill his ranks with regular soldiers, largely indentured servants, freed Black people and new immigrants, for whom a soldier's life was the best of poor options.

Despite the odds, Washington did have some victories, including a surprise Christmas night attack on Hessian soldiers who had been hired by the British. The battle was immortalized (albeit incorrectly) in Emanuel Leutze's 1851 painting *Washington Crossing the Delaware*. The Patriot's successes were turning points: they persuaded France (a longtime British foe) to recognize the United States and sign on as an American ally.

Eventually, with French naval support, Washington won the Battle of Yorktown in Virginia and forced a British surrender in October 1781. Although it would take two more years to sign the paperwork, the American Revolution was over. It was a great victory for the commander in chief, but Washington's joy was tempered with grief; his stepson, Jack, an administrative aide at Yorktown, caught typhus and died the following month.

Our First President

By 1783, George Washington was back at home at Mount Vernon and would have happily stayed there for the rest of his life. He and Martha were raising Jack's children and welcoming visitors who came to Mount Vernon to meet the war hero. Washington enjoyed long rides on his horse to inspect his various properties surrounding Mount Vernon. But again, duty called.

Washington returned to Philadelphia in May 1787 as part of a delegation tasked with revising the Articles of Confederation. They would end up writing an entirely new U.S. Constitution. Washington had been elected head of the Constitutional Convention, and his fellow delegates assumed that Washington would be willing to lead the new nation that he helped create. The first presidential election had no debates or campaigning. At the time, each member of the Electoral College (selected by their respective state) was to cast two votes for president. The person in first place would be president;

Mount Vernon, George Washington's plantation on the Potomac River. *Courtesy of Mount Vernon Ladies' Association.*

the person in second place would be vice president. Washington was elected unanimously by all sixty-nine voters. John Adams, who had most recently served as ambassador to Great Britain, came in second with thirty-four votes.

Although the American Revolution had been won, Washington recognized that the new nation rested on a fragile union. For the most part, a late eighteenth-century resident of the new nation would not have recognized the label "American"—they were Bostonians, Pennsylvanians or perhaps southerners. There was not yet a real concept of an American identity. The biggest challenge facing Washington in the first few years of his presidency was to solidify the power of the federal government without upsetting those who viewed the United States as a loose confederation of states rather than one united nation.

One of the biggest challenges to the new union of states was the issue of money. By the end of the American Revolution, the United States owed an estimated $40 million to its own citizens and another $25 million to overseas creditors, primarily France. Alexander Hamilton, Washington's secretary of the treasury, advocated for the creation of a central bank that would assume the national debts, issue currency and fund national improvement projects. Others, most notably Secretary of State Thomas Jefferson, were in fierce opposition to Hamilton's plan, arguing that many of the southern states had already paid off much of their debt (thanks to enslaved labor) and that a national bank was an overreach of federal power. The debate over the role of a national bank would continue for many decades to come, but in the short term, it was settled by the Compromise of 1790: James Madison and Thomas Jefferson (both Virginians) allowed the federalization of state debt in return for Hamilton's agreement to have a new national capital built near Virginia.

As the first president of the United States, Washington defined the role that others would later fill. He created the presidential cabinet when he needed advice on negotiating treaties with Native American tribes. He began making plans for a national capital that was to be built just north of his home on the Potomac River. And he stepped down after two terms in office, setting that as the future standard.

Views on Slavery

George Washington grew up in homes supported by enslaved workers. Upon his father's death, he inherited the ownership of some of those people. Washington took enslaved manservants with him when he went to work and to war. Enslaved people labored in the presidential mansions in New York and Philadelphia, as well as on his various plantations.

Although Washington spoke about the possibility of a gradual emancipation of the enslaved, he spared no expense in trying to recapture enslaved people who escaped from his plantations. Pennsylvania had passed an emancipation law in 1780 that, among other things, freed the enslaved who could prove residency in the state for at least six months. This impacted Washington during his time in Philadelphia, where he served in Congress and as president. To bypass the law, Washington rotated his enslaved workers between Virginia and Philadelphia throughout his time in the state so that they could never gain their freedom.

By the time Washington retired to Mount Vernon, he had stopped buying enslaved people and refused to sell (i.e., separate) the families who lived on his plantation. At least half of the more than 300 enslaved people at Mount Vernon belonged to Washington's wife's estate, which, under the property laws of the time, he managed for her heirs. Finally, in the summer of 1799, Washington addressed the issue of slavery in his will; upon Martha's death, the 124 people whom Washington enslaved were to be set free. Until that time, none of them were to be sold, and upon their emancipation, those who were too young or old to care for themselves were to be provided for by Washington's heirs. In the end, Martha freed them early, largely because she feared for her own safety after Washington's death.

Retirement

George Washington finally retired to his Mount Vernon home in 1797 and settled into solidifying his legacy. He spent time gathering his letters and other writings and entertaining guests.

On December 12, 1799, Washington went for a ride around Mount Vernon, as he did most days. It was a stormy day, and he came down with what he believed was a cold. Over the next two days, his illness got worse, and Washington complained of a pain in his throat and said he had trouble breathing. What was probably a bacterial infection—easily treated with modern antibiotics—led to Washington's death during the night of December 14, 1799. He was buried at Mount Vernon.

George Washington Historic Sites in Virginia

George Washington Birthplace National Monument
1732 Popes Creek Road, Colonial Beach, VA
804-224-1732 extension 227
nps.gov/gewa

George Washington was born at Popes Creek Plantation on February 22, 1732, and lived there until he was three years old. The land originally belonged to George's great-grandfather. It was operated as a tobacco plantation and was worked by twenty to twenty-five enslaved laborers. The exact location of the house in which George was born is unknown; it is believed the home burned down sometime in the late 1700s. By 1858, when the property was acquired by the state of Virginia, the farm had fallen into ruin.

In the 1920s, a group of women philanthropists lobbied to have the plantation on which Washington was born dedicated as a national monument. They also raised funds and built a Colonial Revival–style model house on the land in celebration of Washington's two hundredth birthday that was to serve as a "living monument" to the president. The house was built on top of what was believed, at the time, to be the ruins of Washington's birthplace. Ongoing archaeological excavations at the site have called this into question. For many years, the 1930s house was interpreted as a reproduction of Washington's birthplace; it is now interpreted to tell the story of the women whose efforts preserved Popes Creek Plantation in the early days of historic preservation.

The site is currently operated by the National Park Service and is open daily. The grounds include the 1930s house and several Colonial-style reproduction outbuildings. The Washington family cemetery is a short drive away. It is strongly recommended that visitors take the ranger-led tour of the 1930s house, which explains the complicated history of the house and plantation.

GEORGE WASHINGTON'S FERRY FARM
268 King's Highway, Fredericksburg, VA
540-370-0732
ferryfarm.org

What is now known as Ferry Farm is the site of George Washington's boyhood home, located across the Rappahannock River from Fredericksburg, Virginia. Washington's father, Augustine, purchased the 580-acre plantation around 1739 and moved his family here in order to be closer to the ironworks in which he had part ownership. Known then as Home Farm, the original plantation was comprised of tobacco, corn, wheat and other crops worked by an estimated twenty enslaved workers. Washington lived there with his family from the time he was six years old until his early twenties. Washington inherited the plantation after his father's death in 1743, and his widowed mother lived on the farm until 1772. In that year, Washington purchased a house for his mother in downtown Fredericksburg and sold the plantation.

The Home Farm plantation passed through many hands over the years, and several buildings were built and torn down there. Eventually, a large portion of the land was sold off to become a housing development. In 1996, when the core property was under threat of retail development, a group of local residents got together to raise funds to protect the property. After years of archaeological excavation, staff members were finally able to locate the remains of the Washington home's foundation in 2004. Over the next several years, the George Washington Foundation, the owner of the property, built a replica of the Washington-era building on top of the original foundation and furnished it with custom-made reproduction furniture. The six-room farmhouse was opened to the public in 2018.

The dining room at George Washington's Ferry Farm, furnished with modern reproductions of period furniture. *Photograph by EagleOne Photography and courtesy of George Washington's Ferry Farm.*

The museum's visitor center tells the story of the archaeological excavations and archival research that informed the construction and interpretation of the replica house. Visitors can also peek into the onsite archaeology lab with exhibits on how objects are cleaned, identified and preserved. Hour-long guided tours of the replica house are offered daily.

GEORGE WASHINGTON'S MOUNT VERNON
3200 Mount Vernon Memorial Highway, Mount Vernon, VA
703-780-2000
mountvernon.org

Mount Vernon was originally built by George Washington's father, Augustine, around 1734 and was likely a modest four-room house. Washington lived here briefly as a child (circa 1735–39) and then as often as possible from 1754 onward. He originally rented the estate from his late half brother Lawrence's wife until she died, and he inherited it in 1761. Washington added on to the house just before his marriage to Martha Custis and again in the 1770s. He also acquired surrounding land and made numerous improvements to the estate. At the time of Washington's death in 1799, Mount Vernon had grown to a three-story, eleven-thousand-square-foot

A guide leads a tour of George Washington's Mount Vernon. *Photograph by Dan Chung and courtesy of Mount Vernon Ladies' Association.*

mansion, and the estate comprised eight thousand acres spread across five farms, a distillery and a gristmill.

The preservation of Mount Vernon is one of the earliest examples of historic preservation in America. After Martha Washington's death in 1802, Mount Vernon was inherited by her nephew. The house remained in the Washington/Custis family, but by the 1850s, the descendants were struggling to maintain the house and it had fallen into disrepair. A group of women, led by Ann Pamela Cunningham, got together and launched an effort to raise money to purchase the house from the family. They called themselves the Mount Vernon Ladies' Association of the Union and had representatives from each of the nation's states. Their efforts were successful, and by 1858, they had raised $200,000 to purchase the mansion and two hundred acres. Philosophies about historic preservation and interpretation have changed over the many years, but the association's goal was to return the house to its circa-1799 appearance and return as many of the family's items to the home as possible. In this, it has been remarkably successful.

George Washington's Mount Vernon currently comprises five hundred acres and includes the mansion, slave quarters, many outbuildings, Washington's tomb, a slave cemetery, a distillery, a gristmill and a demonstration farm. The mansion and a few outbuildings are original; the others are modern re-creations based on original drawings or archaeological excavations. Each year, from April to October, there are costumed interpreters at the farm. There is also an education center and museum with interpretive exhibits about Washington and his times, several films and an interactive exhibit, where visitors can challenge themselves with some of the leadership decisions Washington faced during his career. Highlights of the collection include a key to the Bastille that was given to Washington by Lafayette, original furniture and artwork, a set of Washington's dentures and life-sized models of Washington at various ages with explanations of how they were created.

George Washington's Mount Vernon is open daily. Visitors can take a thirty-minute guided tour of the mansion and additional thematic tours. The hour-long "Enslaved People of Mount Vernon" was a particularly good tour and ended with a moving ceremony at the cemetery where enslaved workers at Mount Vernon are believed to be buried. There is also a free audio tour of the grounds and activities for children and teens available at the orientation center. There is a gift shop and several dining options adjacent to the museum.

GEORGE WASHINGTON'S OFFICE MUSEUM

32 West Cork and Braddock Streets, Winchester, VA
540-662-4412
winchesterhistory.org

This small log building was used as an office by George Washington during the French and Indian War, when he was planning the construction of nearby Fort Loudoun. The building is now operated by the Winchester-

George Washington's Office Museum in Winchester. *Author's photograph.*

Frederick County Historical Society and includes a self-guided exhibit on Washington and the war. Highlights include a lock of Washington's hair and a bench that was recovered from Fort Loudoun before it fell into ruins. The museum is open daily.

MARY WASHINGTON'S HOME

1200 Charles Street, Fredericksburg, VA
540-373-1569
washingtonheritagemuseums.org

George Washington purchased this one-and-a-half story house on a one-acre double lot for his mother in 1772. Located in downtown Fredericksburg, it was closer to the homes of two of her grown children, Betty and Charles, and was much easier to maintain than the larger Home Farm plantation (now George Washington's Ferry Farm). Mary Washington lived in the house with her enslaved staff until her death in 1789 at the age of eighty years old. After her death, Washington sold the house, and subsequent owners added on to the original house. Hour-long guided tours of the house are offered by costumed interpreters daily.

HISTORIC KENMORE

1201 Washington Avenue, Fredericksburg, VA
540-373-3381
kenmore.org

Historic Kenmore was the home of George Washington's sister and her husband, Betty and Colonel Fielding Lewis. The George Washington Foundation offers daily tours of the 1775 Georgian-style house, located in downtown Fredericksburg.

RISING SUN TAVERN

1304 Caroline Street, Fredericksburg, VA
540-371-1494
washingtonheritagemuseums.org

This building was constructed by George Washington's youngest brother, Charles, around 1760 and then operated as a tavern from the 1790s to the 1820s. Guided tours are offered daily.

COLONIAL WILLIAMSBURG

101 Visitor Center Drive, Williamsburg, VA
888-965-7254
colonialwilliamsburg.org

For a broader perspective on life in Virginia on the eve of the American Revolution, a visit to Colonial Williamsburg is essential. This living history museum stretches over three hundred acres and is composed of eighty-eight original buildings, including shops, taverns, government sites and homes. Costumed historical interpreters (including those representing Washington, Jefferson, Madison and Monroe) share their stories at most of the sites, and there is a wide assortment of music, food, animals and activities for visitors of all ages.

Colonial Williamsburg is open daily, and there are a variety of ticket options.

YORKTOWN BATTLEFIELD

Colonial National Historical Park, Yorktown, VA
757-898-2410
nps.gov/york

It was here, in the fall of 1781, that General George Washington led American and French soldiers in the Siege of Yorktown, forcing the surrender of the British troops led by General Charles Cornwallis and eventually bringing to a successful end the American Revolution. The national park site includes a

Volunteers depicting Colonel John Lamb's Second Regiment of the Continental Artillery demonstrate the firing of an eighteen-pounder siege cannon at the Yorktown Battlefield. *U.S. National Park Service.*

visitor center, several historic sites and the battlefield, which is accessible by a self-guided driving tour.

AMERICAN REVOLUTION MUSEUM AT YORKTOWN

200 Water Street, Yorktown, VA
757-253-4838
jyfmuseums.org

This museum of the American Revolution includes exhibits about the war, a Revolutionary-era farm and a re-creation of a Continental Army encampment. The museum is open daily.

OUTSIDE OF VIRGINIA

WASHINGTON MONUMENT

Fifteenth Street and Madison Drive Northwest, Washington, D.C.
877-444-6777
nps.gov/wamo

The 555-foot-tall marble monument to our first president is the tallest structure in Washington, D.C. The construction of the monument began in 1848 and was finally completed in 1884. At the time, it was the tallest structure in the world. Free tickets to ride the elevator to the top of the monument are available online in advance or by calling the phone number above.

PRESIDENT'S HOUSE SITE

Corner of Sixth and Market Streets, Philadelphia, PA
215-965-2305
nps.gov/inde

This memorial marks the site of the three-story brick building that served as the executive mansion from 1790 to 1800. Washington lived there with his family and enslaved staff from 1790 until he left office in 1797. (The two houses he occupied while the national capital was located in New York City

The Washington Monument, the tallest structure in Washington, D.C., overlooking the reflecting pool on the National Mall. *Photograph by Camille Dierksheide.*

have since been demolished.) President John Adams then lived in the house until the national capital was relocated to Washington, D.C. The original building was demolished in the nineteenth century; the memorial re-creates the footprint of the building.

President's House Site is part of Independence National Historical Park and is located next to the Liberty Bell Center. It is open daily, and admission is free.

2

THOMAS JEFFERSON

Our Third President

Fast Facts About Thomas Jefferson

- Third president of the United States.
- Born April 13, 1743; died July 4, 1826.
- Served two terms: 1801–9.
- Married Martha Wayles Skelton (1748–1782) in 1772. Partnered with Sally Hemings (circa 1773–1835) from around 1790 until his death.
- Children with Martha Wayles Skelton: Martha "Patsy" (1772–1836), Jane (1774–1775), a son (1777–1777), Mary "Polly" (1778–1804), Lucy Elizabeth (1780–1781) and another Lucy Elizabeth (1782–1784). Children with Sally Hemings: a child (circa 1790), Harriet (1795–1797), William Beverly (1798–unknown), a daughter (1799–1799), another Harriet (1801–unknown), James Madison (1805–1877) and Thomas Eston (1809–1856).
- Nicknamed the "Sage of Monticello."
- First president inaugurated in Washington, D.C.
- Author of the Declaration of Independence.
- Prior careers: lawyer, planter, diplomat, state legislator, governor, vice president and architect.

Thomas Jefferson, the third president of the United States. *Library of Congress, Prints and Photographs Division.*

ALL ABOUT THOMAS JEFFERSON

More than any of the other Virginia presidents, Thomas Jefferson is a study in contradictions. He was an advocate for religious freedom who believed in forcing Christianity on Native Americans; he was an advocate for small federal government who stretched his role as president to purchase the

Louisiana Territories; and he was an advocate for freedom who enslaved more than six hundred people, including his own biracial children and their mother, Sally Hemings. We know from his writings that he understood that slavery was unsustainable, if not morally wrong. Yet he was either unable or unwilling to give up the material comforts it provided. How does knowing what we do of his personal life and values inform our understanding of the foundational documents of our nation that he authored, including the Declaration of Independence? Can we—should we—separate the public man from the private one?

Early Life

Like most of the Virginia presidents, Thomas Jefferson was born into the elite Virginia planter class and lived a materially comfortable childhood. He was the eldest son of Peter Jefferson, a planter, surveyor and land speculator, and his wife, Jane Randolph Jefferson. Thomas was born on a plantation located just outside of the current city of Charlottesville, Virginia, called Shadwell. When he was a toddler, the Jefferson family moved to Tuckahoe Plantation, a nearby plantation owned by a family friend. He lived at Tuckahoe until the age of seven, and then the family returned to Shadwell. Jefferson had five siblings, including an older sister with developmental disabilities, about whom little is known. Peter Jefferson died when Thomas was fourteen years old and, and as the eldest son, Thomas inherited both his father's real estate and thirty enslaved servants.

Thomas was well educated and enjoyed a life of the mind, with his interests ranging from architecture to natural history and classic literature. As a child, he was educated by tutors and at a small private school. At the age of seventeen, he enrolled at the College of William and Mary in Williamsburg, Virginia. He brought with him his enslaved manservant Jupiter Evans.

Thomas graduated from the College of William and Mary in 1762 and then spent the next five years studying law. He was admitted to the Virginia bar in 1767 and practiced law for the next seven years.

The Eve of Revolution

Thomas Jefferson began his political career in 1769, when he was elected to the Virginia House of Burgesses, the legislative body for the colony. It was from this seat that he witnessed the events leading up to the American Revolution. Like others of his class and station, Jefferson's initial complaints with Great Britain were that the colonists were not being treated as equal British subjects, specifically regarding taxation. Jefferson and others saw their colonial government as being equal to the British Parliament, and thus, they believed they should be subject to only the lawmaking and taxation as decided locally. British Parliament, in contrast, believed that the colonists should have to repay the debts that Great Britain accumulated while defending the colonists during the French and Indian War. It was a fundamental and ultimately unresolvable difference in interpretation of British law.

Jefferson was an early backer of the colonial protests against Great Britain. When the Sons of Liberty dumped crates of tea into Boston Harbor in December 1773, the British Parliament responded by revoking the colonial charter and imposing martial law on the city. Jefferson was not elected to the First Continental Congress (fall 1774), during which the delegates agreed to boycott British goods, but he encouraged his fellow Virginians to support Bostonians in their protests.

On January 1, 1772, Jefferson married Martha Wayles Skelton, a wealthy widow whose young son had died shortly before they met. He brought Martha to live on a plantation near today's Charlottesville, Virginia, that he had inherited from his father. At the time, the grand estate that would become Thomas Jefferson's Monticello was a five-thousand-acre tobacco plantation, and the Jeffersons lived in a small cottage on the grounds. They had their first child, Martha, later that year. Together, the couple had a total of six children, only two of whom, Martha and Mary, born six years later, survived to adulthood.

In 1773, Jefferson's father-in-law John Wayles died. Following the property laws of the time, Jefferson took over the management of a portion of his estate, which included two plantations, more than one hundred enslaved people and thousands of dollars in debt. (Jefferson would never fully settle the debt from his father-in-law, and that, coupled with his own exorbitant spending, would eventually lead to his financial ruin.) Among the enslaved people who were moved to Monticello upon John Wayles's death were Wayles's enslaved mistress, Elizabeth Hemings, and their five children, including an infant daughter, Sally.

Author of the Declaration of Independence

In May 1775, delegates from twelve of the thirteen colonies reconvened in Philadelphia to decide how to respond to the outbreak of war with Great Britain in the colony of Massachusetts. This gathering would become known as the Second Continental Congress and would serve as the government of the colonies throughout the American Revolution. Thomas Jefferson was elected to serve in the Second Continental Congress but missed the first several months of governing in order to care for his ailing wife and newborn daughter, the latter of whom died.

When Jefferson arrived in Philadelphia in the spring of 1776, the Second Continental Congress appointed him to serve on a committee to draft a "Declaration of the Causes and Necessities for Taking Up Arms" against the British. Jefferson spent seventeen days writing the first draft of what would become the Declaration of Independence. In the end, Congress removed or rewrote about one-quarter of Jefferson's draft, most notably a paragraph that Jefferson wrote that blamed Great Britain for the slave trade. The document was ratified on July 4, 1776, officially the first step in the formation of a new nation.

The Declaration of Independence, July 4, 1776. Print from a painting by John Trumbull. *Library of Congress, Prints and Photographs Division.*

Jefferson never fought in the Continental Army. Instead, he returned to Virginia, where he was elected to the Virginia House of Delegates, the lower house of the state legislature. During the next several years, he focused on writing a constitution for the new state of Virginia and revising more than one hundred state laws. Among his accomplishments was a "Bill for Establishing Religious Freedom" for Virginia, which was adopted in 1786 and established that the state government would not provide any financial support for religion.

In June 1779, Jefferson was elected governor of Virginia and served two one-year terms. He refused a third term, largely to return to Monticello, where his wife, Martha, was gravely ill after giving birth to their sixth child. The baby survived, but Martha died in September 1782.

Diplomat to France

The United States and Great Britain signed the Treaty of Paris in 1783, bringing an end to the American Revolutionary War. In June that year, Thomas Jefferson was elected to the Confederation Congress, the governing body of the United States under the 1781 Articles of Confederation, which were written during the war. Jefferson left his children under the care of the enslaved staff at Monticello to serve in Philadelphia. He found the work there a welcome distraction from his grief over his wife's death, so when Congress offered him the opportunity to go to France to advocate for trade and diplomatic relations with Europe, he agreed. He took his eldest daughter, Martha, with him but left his two surviving younger daughters, Mary and Lucy, in Virginia with extended family.

Jefferson spent five years in France (from 1784 to 1789), first as a trade minister and then replacing Benjamin Franklin as minister to France. He enrolled his daughter in a local boarding school and paid for his enslaved servant, James Hemings, to train as a French chef. While in France, Jefferson wrote "Notes on the State of Virginia," an essay about Virginia's nature, history and politics that also offered a race-based justification for slavery.

In May 1787, after receiving word that his two-year-old daughter, Lucy, had died of whooping cough in Virginia, Jefferson sent for his eight-year-old daughter, Mary, to join him in Paris. Mary was accompanied across the Atlantic Ocean by her personal attendant, an enslaved fourteen-year-old Sally Hemings, the sister of James and half-sister of Jefferson's late wife.

Sometime during their time in France, Jefferson began a sexual relationship with Sally. By September 1789, when the family was making plans to return to the United States, sixteen-year-old Sally was pregnant with Jefferson's child. The child was likely born in early 1790 but did not survive very long.

Relationship with Sally Hemings

The true nature of the relationship between Thomas Jefferson and Sally Hemings will never be known, but historians have uncovered evidence that suggests that it was more complicated than their thirty-year age difference and Hemings's enslaved status might suggest. While living in France, Hemings was legally free and could have walked away from Jefferson's employment with no negative repercussions. She could have found a job as a servant in the home of a wealthy Parisian family or even gone into business with her brother, a talented chef.

Yet in the fall of 1789, a pregnant teenaged Hemings opted instead for an enslaved life in Virginia. According to the Hemings family's history, she agreed to return to Mount Vernon after exacting a promise from Jefferson that neither she nor her children would have to work hard labor at Monticello and that all her children would be freed from slavery when they reached the age of twenty-one. Historian Annette Gordon-Reed has argued that this is among the evidence that suggests an ongoing and mutually affectionate relationship between the two people of vastly different statuses. Gordon-Reed also emphasizes the tight bonds among the extended Hemings family at Monticello as a draw for Sally Hemings's return to Virginia.

Over the next two decades, Jefferson fathered six additional children with Hemings, four of whom survived to adulthood. His children lived among the other enslaved people at Monticello. His sons were trained in carpentry and his daughter in handiwork. Jefferson apparently kept his promise; none of his children were forced into hard labor, and all four were freed by the time they became adults (two informally when they reached the age of twenty-one and two in Jefferson's will upon his death). Hemings was never legally freed; after Jefferson's death, she was "given her time" by Jefferson's daughter. This was an informal freeing that was sometimes done for favored enslaved staff when they became too old to work. Hemings, then about fifty-three years old, left Monticello to live with one of her sons in Charlottesville, where she remained until her own death.

Our Third President

Upon his return to the United States in 1790, Thomas Jefferson was appointed secretary of state under George Washington. During his time in Washington's cabinet, Jefferson sparred frequently with Secretary of the Treasury Alexander Hamilton over the role and power of the federal government. Jefferson believed in a limited central government, envisioning instead a nation of small farmers loosely organized into the United States. Hamilton, in contrast, believed in a powerful federal government and the centralization of national finances. Their two differing belief systems would eventually become the first political parties in the United States: Hamilton's Federalists and Jefferson's Democratic-Republicans. They did, however, reach a compromise in 1790, when Jefferson and U.S. representative James Madison agreed to support Hamilton's national banking system in exchange for Hamilton's endorsement of building the new nation's permanent capital in the South, specifically on the Potomac River in Virginia.

After a brief hiatus back at Monticello, Jefferson set his sights on higher office and ran against John Adams in the 1796 presidential election. Jefferson came in second, delegating him to serve as Adams's vice president. At the time, the vice president had no specific role other than to oversee the Senate, and Jefferson's four years serving as vice president were uneventful.

In 1800, Jefferson ran again for the presidency. This time, he tied with former U.S. senator Aaron Burr, each receiving seventy-three electoral votes. The House of Representatives broke the tie and selected Jefferson, largely because of Alexander Hamilton's endorsement of his former rival. When Jefferson took office the following March, it was the first peaceful transition of power from one political party to another. In 1804, Congress passed the Twelfth Amendment, which directed electors to cast separate ballots for president and vice president, ensuring that this situation would not occur again.

Among Jefferson's goals as president was the reduction of the national debt. He repealed all internal taxes, reduced the size of the civil service and argued against a standing army and navy. But Jefferson also believed in the importance of international trade and was happy to spend money to make sure that could continue. In 1801, he sent a naval squadron to the Mediterranean Sea in order to keep trade open in that area. Two years later, he authorized the purchase of all of Louisiana in order to keep the Port of New Orleans open for trade.

The Louisiana Purchase

In 1800, French leader Napoleon Bonaparte acquired Louisiana from Spain as part of his attempt to establish a new colonial presence in North America. Thomas Jefferson was concerned that France might cut off America's access to trading via the Port of New Orleans, so in 1803, he sent diplomat James Monroe and Virginia governor Robert Livingston to discuss the purchase of the port from France. By then, the new French Republic was dealing with an uprising of the enslaved population in Haiti and an outbreak of yellow fever among its troops, and it needed money to fund its ongoing battle with Great Britain. The American diplomats asked for the Port of New Orleans; Bonaparte offered all of Louisiana.

Jefferson, in a move that belied all his talk of reducing federal spending, signed treaties to purchase more than eight hundred thousand square miles from France for $15 million. The Louisiana Purchase increased the size

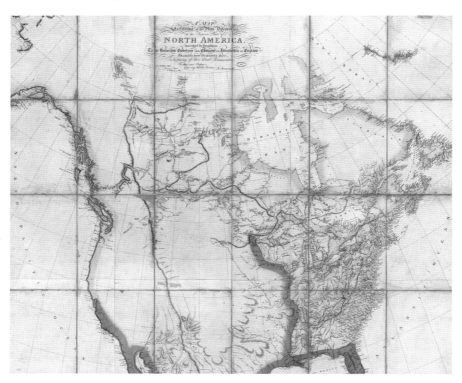

A map of North America in 1802. *Library of Congress, Geography and Map Division, Louisiana: European Explorations and the Louisiana Purchase.*

of the United States by 140 percent. Upon Jefferson's request, Congress agreed to secretly fund a cross-country expedition to explore and document the new territory. The Lewis and Clark Expedition departed in May 1804 and returned three years later. Along the way, Meriwether Lewis, William Clark, their Shoshone guide Sacagawea and the rest of their crew mapped a westward route to the Pacific Ocean, documented natural resources and began trade and diplomatic relationships with the Native Americans they met along the way.

Jefferson was less successful in his diplomatic relations across the Atlantic Ocean. Both Great Britain and France—themselves at war with each other—regularly attacked American ships in the Atlantic and captured both goods and sailors. In 1807, Jefferson persuaded Congress to pass an Embargo Act, prohibiting trade with either country until the attacks ended. The embargo ended up having little impact on the Europeans but decimated the American economy. Congress was forced to repeal the act two years later, forcing Jefferson's successor to figure out how to deal with the British and French once he took office.

Retirement

In March 1809, after his friend and successor James Madison was inaugurated as president, Thomas Jefferson left the White House and retired to his Virginia plantation. He spent the next several years organizing his papers and hosting numerous visitors to Monticello. It was during this period that he got the

Monticello, Thomas Jefferson's plantation outside of Charlottesville. © *Thomas Jefferson Foundation at Monticello.*

nickname the "Sage of Monticello." In 1814, Jefferson sold his scholarly book collection to Congress to replace those books that had been destroyed when the British set fire to Washington, D.C., during the War of 1812. His six thousand books would be the beginning of the modern Library of Congress.

Jefferson also cultivated interests in architecture and landscape design. He had designed and redesigned his home at Monticello before retiring there and had designed several other public buildings, including the Virginia State Capitol in Richmond. When the Virginia legislature authorized the creation of a college in Virginia, Jefferson was pleased to design its central campus and buildings. The University of Virginia opened in 1825, not far from his home in Charlottesville, Virginia.

Views on Slavery

During his lifetime, Thomas Jefferson enslaved more than six hundred people, making him the second-largest slaveholder in Virginia at the time. His enslaved workers labored at Monticello, in the White House and on his other plantations. They worked in the fields, in the houses and in several small factories that he set up at Monticello. Several of the enslaved workers at Monticello were members of his own extended family and included his four biracial children and his late wife Martha's half-siblings by her father (including Sally Hemings).

Although he argued against the international slave trade and his 1785 essay "Notes on the State of Virginia" argued for the gradual emancipation of the enslaved, he only freed two enslaved people during his lifetime. Although they were not legally freed, he also allowed two of his enslaved children to "escape" without pursuing their return. Jefferson directed that five enslaved people should be freed upon his death; two of them were his children, and the others were extended family members.

Jefferson spent most of his retirement deep in debt. He had spent a small fortune on his various architectural and intellectual pursuits at a time when his plantations were declining in productivity. After his death, his surviving daughter Martha was forced to sell off Monticello and most of the enslaved staff to pay his debts.

On July 3, 1826, Jefferson fell sick with a fever. He died the next day, the fiftieth anniversary of the ratification of the Declaration of Independence. Former president John Adams died five hours later. Jefferson was buried at Monticello.

Thomas Jefferson Historic Sites in Virginia

Shadwell Plantation
38°0.906′North, 78°24.948′West
Route 250, Albemarle County, VA

Thomas Jefferson's birthplace is no longer standing. A historical marker noting its location can be found on Route 250, east of Charlottesville.

Tuckahoe Plantation
12601 River Road, Richmond, VA
804-774-1614
visithistorictuckahoe.com

The home where Thomas Jefferson lived between the ages of two and seven is presently operated as a wedding venue. Self-guided tours of the grounds are available daily, and guided tours are available on select Saturdays.

Monticello
1050 Monticello Loop, Charlottesville, VA
434-984-9800
monticello.org

Monticello was Thomas Jefferson's mountaintop plantation outside of Charlottesville from 1764 until his death in 1826. He inherited the land from his father and spent the next two decades building and then rebuilding the estate's home. Jefferson was a self-taught architect and designed many of the notable elements of Monticello himself, modeling them after classical Roman architecture.

The construction of the first house at Monticello began in 1768 and was paused when Jefferson left for France in 1784. The original home had only eight rooms and outbuildings. In 1790, Jefferson began planning a renovation of Monticello, incorporating design elements he had seen abroad. These renovations began in 1794 and were largely complete by the time Jefferson retired to Monticello in 1809. Most of the work on the house was completed by enslaved staff who were trained by skilled craftsmen whom Jefferson hired. The renovated home at Monticello included its notable dome, forty-

Thomas Jefferson's study at Monticello. © *Thomas Jefferson Foundation at Monticello.*

three rooms and several unusual architectural features. Eventually, Jefferson's widowed sister and his eldest daughter and her family would live with him at Monticello.

Jefferson's land holdings included Monticello and three adjacent plantations, Tufton, Lego and Shadwell (his childhood home), totaling about five thousand acres. The plantations initially grew tobacco for export and then wheat and rye. In addition to the farms, Jefferson set up several small industries at Monticello—blacksmithing, carpentry, nail-making, et cetera—in order to support the construction of his mansion and to keep the plantation as self-sufficient as possible. At any one time, Monticello was supported by around 130 enslaved farm workers, house servants and skilled craftsmen.

After Jefferson's death, Monticello (and all but a very few enslaved staff) were sold off to pay his debts. The Thomas Jefferson Memorial Foundation was established in 1923 and purchased the house and 650 acres of the former plantation. It embarked on a restoration of the mansion, and the first paying visitors to Monticello arrived the following year.

Monticello currently comprises about 2,500 acres and includes Jefferson's mansion, various outbuildings and dependencies, the Jefferson family's cemetery, a visitor's center and an educational center. Several dependencies and enslaved staff homes have been restored or re-created; others include exhibits about life on the plantation. Of particular interest in the house is the entrance hall, which includes original and replica artifacts from the Lewis and Clark Expedition, natural history specimens and a unique Jefferson-designed clock that displays not just the time but also the days of the week. Throughout the house are some of the period gadgets that Jefferson enjoyed collecting, including a two-pen copying machine and a dumb waiter that was used to bring wine from the basement wine cellar.

Monticello offers several specialized and seasonal tours, including a behind-the-scenes tour, a family-friendly tour and a tour focused on the enslaved staff at Monticello. Visitors can also purchase a ticket to tour the grounds and exhibits alone. There are also a variety of walking trails on the property.

Poplar Forest

1542 Bateman Bridge Road, Forest, VA
434-525-1806
poplarforest.org

Poplar Forest was Thomas Jefferson's retreat, located in an area that was then a two-day carriage ride from Monticello. The Jeffersons inherited the land after the death of Martha's father in 1773. Jefferson designed and supervised the construction of the octagonal house, beginning in 1806. By 1809, he was visiting the house several times a year, staying for as long as two months. The property was maintained by eleven to one hundred enslaved staff.

After Jefferson's death, his grandson sold the house, and it remained in the same family for the next one hundred–plus years. In the mid-1840s, a fire destroyed the original house, and its owners rebuilt a remodeled house. In 1983, the house and fifty surrounding acres were purchased by a group of local citizens, who opened the remodeled house for tours. Beginning in 1991, the Corporation for Jefferson's Poplar Forest began a restoration of the house to return it to Jefferson's original design. The project is currently ongoing.

Guided tours of Poplar Forest are offered daily from mid-March through December; self-guided tours are offered during winter weekends.

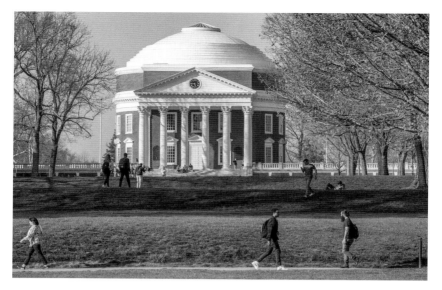

Students on the lawn of the University of Virginia's rotunda, designed by Thomas Jefferson. *Photograph by Sanjay Suchak/UVA University Communications.*

UNIVERSITY OF VIRGINIA

1826 University Avenue, Charlottesville, VA
434-924-7969
rotunda.virginia.edu

The rotunda at the University of Virginia was designed by Thomas Jefferson and built between 1822 and 1828. It was modeled after the Roman Pantheon and designed to have a central library flanked by classrooms and student rooms. The rotunda is open daily, and free tours are offered daily during the academic year.

VIRGINIA STATE CAPITOL

1000 Bank Street, Richmond, VA
804-698-1788
virginiacapitol.gov

The Virginia State Capitol was designed by Thomas Jefferson in 1785, with help from French architect Charles-Louis Clerisseau. The building was completed in 1798. Guided tours of the building are offered daily.

OUTSIDE OF VIRGINIA

JEFFERSON MEMORIAL
16 East Basin Drive Southwest, Washington, D.C.
nps.gov/thje

A nineteen-foot-tall statue of Thomas Jefferson overlooks the Washington Tidal Basin and is modeled after Jefferson's designs at Monticello and the University of Virginia. It was dedicated in 1943 on the two hundredth anniversary of Jefferson's birth. The monument is open daily.

A statue of Thomas Jefferson in the Jefferson Memorial. *Carol M. Highsmith Archive, Library of Congress, Prints and Photographs Division.*

3

JAMES MADISON

Our Fourth President

FAST FACTS ABOUT JAMES MADISON

- Fourth president of the United States.
- Born March 16, 1751; died June 28, 1836.
- Served two terms: 1809–17.
- Married Dolley Payne Todd (1768–1849) in 1794.
- Stepchild: John Payne Todd (1792–1852).
- Nicknamed the "Father of the Constitution" and "Architect of the Bill of Rights."
- Author of the U.S. Constitution.
- Prior careers: state legislator, congressman and secretary of state.

ALL ABOUT JAMES MADISON

James Madison, the fourth president of the United States, is best known for being the intellectual force behind the creation of the U.S. Constitution and its adoption as the rule of the land. While the government that Madison envisioned is not exactly what was agreed on during what is now known as the Constitutional Convention (May–September 1787), most of his ideas regarding a strong centralized power, a three-part federal government and

James Madison, the fourth president of the United States. *Library of Congress, Prints and Photographs Division.*

proportional representation in Congress made their way into the final Constitution. And in this, Madison led the creation of a wholly new form of government, one that continues to serve the needs of a vastly larger, more diverse and more complicated nation over two hundred years later— or does it?

Early Life

James Madison was born in Port Conway, Virginia, at the home of his maternal grandmother. He grew up on his paternal family's plantation in Orange County, Montpelier. Both of his parents, James Madison Sr. and Eleanor Conway Madison, were from wealthy Virginia planter families. His grandmother was a sibling of the father of future president Zachary Taylor.

As the eldest son of twelve children (seven of whom lived to adulthood), James knew from an early age that he would inherit the family plantation. Yet throughout his life, James was less interested in farm management and more invested in a life of the mind. His parents supported his intellectual aspirations and, in fact, saw that all their children—both the boys and girls—received a basic book-based education.

James was tutored at home until the age of eleven, when he was sent to a boarding school near Richmond, where he remained until the age of sixteen. Two years later, James enrolled in the College of New Jersey (now Princeton University), where he completed his degree in just two years. He then remained at Princeton for an additional year for advanced study. He apparently enjoyed the intellectual and social life in New Jersey and likely would have remained there had his father not called him back to Virginia. James returned home in 1772 to tutor his younger siblings and begin the study of law with a mind to eventually enter politics.

Entering the Political Arena

James Madison came into adulthood in the heart of the American Revolution, and many young men his age entered the service. But Madison had been a sickly child and suffered from "spells," likely a form of epilepsy, which precluded a military career. Instead, he set his sights on a political career. At the age of twenty-three, he purchased two hundred acres of land from his father so that, as a white male landowner, he would be eligible to vote and hold office.

Madison's political career began in 1776, when he elected to the Fifth Virginia Convention, the interim legislative body for Virginia, which met from May 6 to July 5 that year in Williamsburg. It was at this convention that Virginia formally declared itself independent from Great Britain and wrote the state's first constitution. Madison served on the committee responsible for writing a bill of rights for the state. Inspired perhaps by the religious diversity he had encountered at Princeton, Madison successfully argued for including language in the bill that would grant not only religious tolerance but also religious freedom for all citizens of Virginia. The Virginia Declaration of Rights would later serve as a model for the U.S. Bill of Rights.

Having had a taste of the urbane life of Williamsburg, Madison was loathe to return to his father's plantation. He ran for the Virginia state legislature but lost, likely because he refused to participate in the tradition of providing alcoholic beverages to poll-goers on election day. He instead served a year in the Virginia governor's office, launching a lifelong friendship with Governor Thomas Jefferson. In 1779, Madison was elected to represent Virginia in the Continental Congress and served three one-year terms in the provisional United States government. He was then elected to the Virginia House of Delegates, where he served until 1787. During this time, he continued to advocate for religious freedom and began building a coalition to reform the Articles of Confederation.

Written by the Second Continental Congress (1775–1781) and ratified in 1781, the Articles of Confederation served as the law of the land until it was superseded by the U.S. Constitution in 1789. The government created under the articles was a loose alliance of thirteen states with a weak central government. The only federal institution was Congress, which was composed of two to seven delegates from each state, but each state got just one vote on legislative matters. The Confederation Congress was empowered to declare war, raise an army and sign treaties, but it did not have the power to tax states. This became an increasing problem throughout the American Revolution, as Congress struggled to clothe, feed and pay soldiers. It was also a problem after peace, as Congress struggled to figure out how to pay war debts.

Madison and others believed that the United States need a stronger central government in order to survive. Madison spent several months in 1786 and 1787 reading everything he could about governments around the world and throughout history to draft a design for a new government. He also worked behind the scenes to persuade the states to send delegates to a convention to discuss reforms to the Articles of Confederation. All but Rhode Island would eventually agree. The group would meet in Philadelphia in the same hall where the Declaration of Independence had been written.

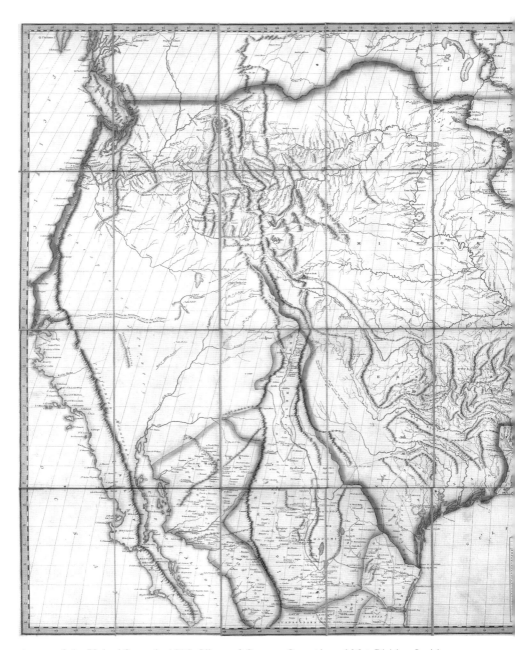

A map of the United States in 1816. *Library of Congress, Geography and Map Division, Louisiana: European Explorations and the Louisiana Purchase.*

A New Constitution

Fifty-five delegates met in Philadelphia's Independence Hall in the spring and summer of 1787 to discuss revising the Articles of Confederation. But very quickly, it became clear that some delegates planned on more than revisions. Virginia governor Edmund Randolph presented Madison's plan—what came to be known as the Virginia Plan—which called for replacing the Articles of Confederation with a wholly new constitution and form of government.

After months of discussion and debate, what emerged was Madison's plan with some modifications and a new government comprising three branches—executive, legislative and judicial—each of which would serve to check the other branches. Congress would be divided into two branches: one in which each state would have equal representation and one in which representation would be determined by each state's population. Madison settled a north/south debate over representation with a compromise that said enslaved people would be counted as three-fifths of a person when determining a state's representation. (Although, of course, the enslaved themselves would not be permitted to vote.) Delegates agreed to the new United States Constitution in September 1787.

After delegates agreed on the new Constitution, it still needed to be ratified by at least nine states in order to go into effect. When there appeared to be hesitancy among some states, Madison joined with Alexander Hamilton and John Jay in writing a series of essays arguing in support of the new Constitution. Those essays, first published in a New York newspaper, came to be known as the Federalist Papers, and they were successful in convincing the public to support the Constitution. It was ratified by the mandatory nine states by 1788 and went into effect the following year.

In 1789, Madison was elected to the new United States House of Representatives and served for the next eight years. He continued to advocate for religious freedom and drafted the first ten amendments to the Constitution, which enumerated the citizen rights that the new federal government could not infringe upon. Those ten amendments became the Bill of Rights, ratified in December 1791.

In the spring of 1794, while living in Philadelphia, James Madison met a twenty-six-year-old widow named Dolley Payne Todd and her young son. Todd had been raised a Quaker, and her Quaker husband and infant daughter had died in a yellow fever outbreak the previous fall. Madison had previously been engaged to a sixteen-year-old in 1783, but she had broken off the engagement to marry someone closer to her own age. Madison was determined to not let another love escape, and the couple were wed in the fall. James, Dolley and her son, Payne, lived in Philadelphia until 1797, when they returned home to Montpelier in Virginia. When Madison's father died in 1801, he inherited the home, plantation and enslaved staff.

Views on Slavery

Like many of his contemporaries, James Madison apparently had mixed feelings about the institution of slavery. Although he wrote against slavery on several occasions, he skirted addressing the issue directly in Congress, fearing that it would alienate his fellow southerners. Madison himself was dependent on the labor of the enslaved staff at Montpelier his entire life. Enslaved staff served him during his childhood, while he was at college in Philadelphia and while he lived in the White House and at home in Virginia.

Montpelier, James Madison's plantation in Orange County. *Photograph by Jennifer Wilkoski and courtesy of Montpelier, a National Trust Historic Site.*

In fact, Madison's very ability to engage in politics was built on the backs of the enslaved men, women and children who labored at his family plantation. The sale of tobacco and other crops from his Virginia plantation paid for his room and board while he served in Congress and supplemented his presidential salary. Although Madison attempted to raise additional funds through land speculation, he was never able to support himself without depending on the labor of enslaved people.

During his lifetime, more than one hundred people were enslaved by Madison at Montpelier, his Virginia plantation. None of the enslaved people were freed during Madison's lifetime or in his will. In her book *The Other Madisons: The Lost History of a President's Black Family*, Betty Kearse presents evidence that Madison may have fathered a child with one of the enslaved women at Montpelier and subsequently sold the child away from the plantation. Later in his life, Madison embraced the idea of building a colony in Africa for freed Black people and served as the president of the American Colonization Society for several years.

Our Fourth President and the War of 1812

In 1801, Thomas Jefferson entered the White House as our third president and asked his friend James Madison to serve as his secretary of state. Much of Madison's time during the next eight years was spent dealing with France and Great Britain, which were both complicating America's trade with Europe. The two countries were at war and refused to recognize the United States' neutrality. In 1807, Madison argued for Congress to pass an Embargo Act to prohibit American trade with Europe, hoping that it would cause harm to France and Great Britain and force them to negotiate with the United States. Instead, the embargo damaged the American economy, and several states flatly refused to comply. Congress was forced to reverse the embargo two years later.

Despite his ongoing struggles with France and Great Britain, Madison easily won the 1808 presidential election against Federalist Charles Cotesworth and became the fourth president of the United States. During the next eight years, Madison saw the new nation through its largest war since the Revolution and continued his efforts to establish the legitimacy of the United States in international affairs.

After Madison's election, problems with Great Britain escalated. British ships regularly intercepted American trading vessels and forced their seamen into the Royal Navy. In addition, Madison believed that the British were

A View of the Presidents House in the City of Washington After the Conflagration of the 24ᵗʰ August, 1814. During the War of 1812, the British set fire to much of Washington, including the White House. *Library of Congress, Prints and Photographs Division.*

stirring up Native American revolts in the western territories, although the expansion of American settlers onto indigenous land was more likely to blame. Things finally came to a head in June 1812, and Congress declared war on Great Britain.

Madison and others believed that what became known as the War of 1812 would be short-lived, but it went on for more than two years. Although Great Britain had several early victories, the United States was successful in battles in the Northwest Territories, thanks in part to the efforts of future president William Henry Harrison. In August 1814, Great Britain had a crushing symbolic victory when four thousand British troops stormed the nation's capital and set fire to the White House. A few days later, American and British troops sparred outside of Baltimore in a battle that was immortalized by Francis Scott Key in what became the United States' national anthem, "The Star-Spangled Banner."

In the end, Great Britain agreed to settle with the United States in order to restore trade between the two countries. On December 24, 1814, Great Britain signed the Treaty of Ghent, ending the war and basically returning everything to the status quo that existed before the war. Although the war was technically a draw, Madison's supporters spun the story that the United States had successfully stood up to the most powerful nation in the world and reaffirmed its independence.

Retirement

In March 1817, James Madison left the White House and retired to Montpelier, his plantation home in Virginia. In 1826, he served as rector of Thomas Jefferson's University of Virginia. In 1829, a seventy-eight-year-old Madison was invited to serve as a delegate to revise Virginia's state constitution. He was the only attendee who had also attended in 1776.

Madison's health deteriorated in the last few years of his life. He died of congestive heart failure at Montpelier on June 28, 1836, at the age of eighty-five. He was buried at Montpelier.

JAMES MADISON HISTORIC SITES IN VIRGINIA

PORT CONWAY/BELLE GROVE PLANTATION

17200 James Madison Parkway, Port Conway, VA
540-621-7340
bellegroveplantation.com

The home where James Madison was born no longer stands; a historical marker identifies the location. The property on which the house stood is presently operated as a bed-and-breakfast.

JAMES MADISON'S MONTPELIER

11350 Constitution Highway, Montpelier Station, VA
540-672-2728
montpelier.org

In 1723, James Madison's grandfather Ambrose Madison acquired five thousand acres of land on what was then the western frontier of Virginia. He sent enslaved workers west to clear the land for a tobacco plantation and eventually built a house for his family. Ambrose died shortly after moving to the plantation, and three enslaved workers were convicted of his murder; one was executed for the crime. Ambrose's widow never remarried, and eventually the plantation passed to her eldest son, James Madison (later James Madison Sr.). The oldest part of the current Montpelier house dates to circa 1764 and was built by James Madison Sr. It was this house in which the future U.S. president and his siblings were raised.

The dining room of James Madison's Montpelier. *Photograph by Larry Bouterie and courtesy of Montpelier, a National Trust Historic Site.*

In 1797, James Madison returned to Montpelier and, knowing that he would eventually inherit the plantation, had an addition built on to the home for his own little family. The addition effectively turned the house into a duplex. After James Madison Sr.'s death in 1801, Madison began a project to unite the house, which was eventually completed in 1812.

The Madisons lived in the house during James Madison's retirement and until his death in 1836. Dolley Madison struggled financially after her husband's death and was eventually forced to sell the plantation in 1844. The house then went through a series of owners until it was purchased by William du Pont (the son of the du Pont company's founder) in 1901. The du Pont family doubled the size of the house and made several major renovations during the eighty years they owned the house. William's daughter, Marion du Pont Scott, added an equestrian training center to the estate, which remains today. After her death, the house came under the ownership of the National Trust for Historic Preservation, which owns it today.

After several years of study, the National Trust for Historic Preservation embarked on a massive project to restore Montpelier to its state during the period of James Madison's retirement (1817–1836). The project involved removing many of the additions that had been made over the years and restoring or re-creating historic architectural features.

James Madison's Montpelier currently comprises the main house, re-created outbuildings and slave cabins, the Madison family and slave cemeteries and a visitor's center. The National Trust for Historic Preservation also continues its archaeological work, and visitors can watch and even participate in ongoing digs. The visitor's center includes a gallery with information about the du Pont family and an installation of one of Marion du Pont Scott's rooms that was removed during the restoration. The basement of the house includes several exhibits about slavery at Montpelier and an award-winning 2017 film about the legacy of slavery. The estate also includes several re-created outbuildings, with exhibits about the enslaved people who lived and worked there. There is also an archaeology lab, where visitors can learn about the discoveries archaeologists have made at Montpelier over the years.

James Madison's Montpelier is open daily, and several guided tours are available, including one that focuses on the enslaved staff. Highlights of the hourlong general house tour include Madison's dining room, study and bedroom.

JAMES MADISON MUSEUM OF ORANGE COUNTY HERITAGE
129 Caroline Street, Orange, VA
540-672-1776
thejamesmadisonmuseum.net

This six-thousand-square-foot museum includes an eclectic collection of exhibits about the history of Orange County from prehistoric times through the nineteenth century. The museum is located in a former trucking business with a huge garage that currently holds a circa-1733 tenant house that was moved from another location in Orange County and an assortment of farm equipment and historic cars. The main hall features exhibits on the two presidents who were born in Orange County: James Madison and Zachary Taylor. The museum is open daily and is self-guided.

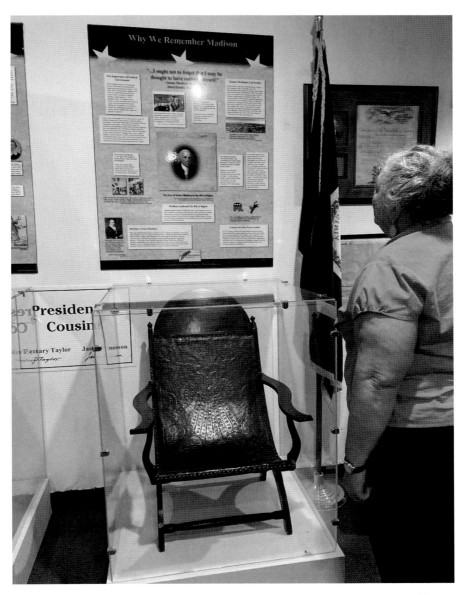

A visitor viewing the exhibits at the James Madison Museum. *Courtesy of the James Madison Museum of Orange County Heritage.*

OUTSIDE OF VIRGINIA

THE OCTAGON MUSEUM
1799 New York Avenue Northwest, Washington, D.C.
202-626-7439
architectsfoundation.org

This building served as the Madisons' home for six months after the British burned the White House during the War of 1812. The house was originally built for a wealthy Washington, D.C. family and is one of the oldest private homes in the city. The American Institute of Architects currently owns and operates the house as a museum and exhibit space. It is open daily and includes a tour and changing exhibits.

The Octagon Museum, the building that served as James Madison's home for six months during the War of 1812. *Photograph by Camille Dierksheide.*

4

JAMES MONROE

Our Fifth President

FAST FACTS ABOUT JAMES MONROE

- Fifth president of the United States.
- Born April 28, 1758; died July 4, 1831.
- Served two terms: 1817–25.
- Married Elizabeth Kortright (1768–1830) in 1786.
- Children: Eliza (1786–1840), James Spence (1799–1800) and Maria Hester (1802–1850).
- Best known for the Monroe Doctrine.
- Last president to have fought as an officer during the American Revolution.
- Prior careers: lawyer, soldier, congressman and diplomat.

ALL ABOUT JAMES MONROE

James Monroe's presidency marked the end of an era. He was the last of the original founding fathers, the last U.S. president to have fought during the American Revolution and the last of the quartet of Virginia-born presidents who so greatly shaped the early republic. Monroe's two terms as president— which included firming up the nation's borders and declaring the Americas

James Monroe, the fifth president of the United States. *Library of Congress, Prints and Photographs Division.*

closed to colonization—began the shift of the federal government's focus from Europe to the West. His Monroe Doctrine also promised that the United States would stay out of European conflicts. What might the world look like today had we kept that promise?

Early Life

James Monroe was born on April 28, 1758, to Spence and Elizabeth Jones Monroe. His parents were among the lower ranks of the planter class in colonial Virginia and owned a five-hundred-acre plantation called Monroe Hall on a tributary of the Potomac River in Westmoreland County, Virginia. His father also worked as a cabinetmaker. James had four siblings: an older sister and three younger brothers. When James was a teenager, both of his parents died within two years of each other, and he inherited Monroe Hall. His uncle Joseph Jones took over the management of the family's estate and the role of surrogate parent to James and his siblings. His uncle also encouraged James to attend the College of William and Mary in Williamsburg, Virginia, where most of the children of wealthy planters studied and made the connections that would serve them in their business and political careers for the rest of their lives.

James enrolled at the College of William and Mary in 1774, not long after the British Parliament closed the Port of Boston in response to the Boston Tea Party the previous year. By September, the First Continental Congress was meeting in Philadelphia, and Williamsburg was wrapped up in revolutionary fervor. James joined in and left college in the spring of 1776 to enlist in the Third Virginia Infantry Regiment. He was just seventeen years old and would serve in the military for the next six years, eventually earning the rank of colonel.

The American Revolution

The Third Virginia joined George Washington's Continental Army in the fall of 1776, and James Monroe fought under Washington for the rest of the year. Monroe's regiment was present at the infamous Christmas night attack on a troop of sleeping Hessian soldiers, the event misdepicted in Emanuel Leutze's 1851 painting *Washington Crossing the Delaware*. Rather than being in the boat with Washington, as depicted in the painting, Monroe led his troops across the Delaware River ahead of Washington and guarded the road to make sure no one stumbled upon the American troops. Monroe was wounded by a musket ball to the shoulder in the following Battle of Trenton and was promoted to captain for his bravery.

After recovering from his injury, Monroe fought in the Battle of Brandywine Creek (September 1777) and survived the brutally cold winter of 1777–78 at Washington's Valley Forge encampment. In 1779, as the war began to turn in the favor of the Patriots and their French allies, Monroe was made aide to then–Virginia governor Thomas Jefferson. This began a lifelong friendship between the two men. Jefferson mentored Monroe in the study of law, a career that Monroe would pursue off and on for the next few years.

In the Footsteps of Jefferson and Madison

Despite his success as a soldier, James Monroe's true passion was politics. In this, he would follow in the footsteps of his mentor Thomas Jefferson and friend James Madison, often literally filling the positions that they vacated. Monroe began his political career in the Virginia House of Delegates in 1782. He was then elected to the Confederation Congress, the governing body for the United States under the Articles of Confederation, and served until 1786.

While in New York, Monroe met Elizabeth Kortright, the daughter of a well-to-do New York merchant. The couple married in 1786 and eventually had three children: two daughters born sixteen years apart and a son born in between who died as an infant.

After Congress wrapped up for its 1786 session, the Monroes relocated to Fredericksburg, Virginia, where James opened a law office, and they rented a home from his uncle. Like his predecessors, Monroe had learned that the compensation paid to public servants did not cover one's expenses, and he hoped to earn enough practicing law to sustain his political ambitions. Like Jefferson and Madison before him, this would be a lifelong struggle.

Monroe was not part of the group that wrote the U.S. Constitution but was a delegate to the Virginia convention called to ratify it in 1788. Monroe voted against the ratification of the Constitution, arguing that the federal government should be given the power to take control of state militias when needed (something that would come to pass many years later) and that the Constitution needed a bill of rights to be added before ratification. In the end, Virginia ratified the document, and Monroe accepted the Constitution once it was passed.

Monroe ran against his friend James Madison for a seat in the first U.S. Senate under the new Constitution but lost. In 1790, a spot opened after the death of another Virginia senator, and after his election, Monroe served in Congress for four years.

A statue of James Monroe at Highland, his plantation outside of Charlottesville. *Library of Congress, Prints and Photographs Division.*

French Diplomat

In 1794, President George Washington asked James Monroe to serve as a minister to France. It was a particularly difficult moment in U.S. international relations, as the new nation tried to establish its legitimacy with the major European powers while remaining neutral regarding the ongoing conflict between Great Britain and France. Monroe was given the tasks of smoothing over relations with France (which believed that the United States should have been more supportive during the French Revolution) and negotiating the United States' access to the Port of New Orleans from France. Monroe was successful on both fronts—too successful. Washington called him home after just two years, because his close relationship with France was threatening the United States' relationship with Great Britain. Unknown to him, Monroe would have another chance in France just a few years later.

Upon his return from Europe, Monroe was elected governor of Virginia, following in the footsteps of friends Jefferson and Madison. He held that position from 1799 through 1801. In August 1800, Monroe received word of a planned rebellion of the enslaved outside of Richmond, Virginia. He ordered militia to the area to patrol the plantations there. No uprising occurred, but dozens of enslaved workers were arrested, and a total of twenty-six people were executed. In the wake of the event, the Virginia General Assembly passed even stricter laws to control both free and enslaved Black Americans.

By 1801, Thomas Jefferson had been elected president and was increasingly concerned about the United States having continued access to the Port of New Orleans, which Jefferson viewed as necessary for trade in the West. In January 1803, Jefferson asked Monroe to go to France to work with Virginia governor Robert Livingston to negotiate the purchase of New Orleans and the western portion of Florida. Napoleon Bonaparte, looking to raise money for his war with Great Britain, offered all the Louisiana Territories to the United States. This was an offer that Jefferson, through Monroe, readily accepted. The issue of Florida, which was still owned by Spain, would have to wait several years for a resolution.

After his success in negotiating the Louisiana Purchase, Monroe was deployed to Great Britain and then to Spain (to try to negotiate for Florida) and then back to Great Britain to try to stop the ongoing interception of U.S. ships and the impressment of American sailors into the Royal Navy. None of those diplomatic posts were terribly successful, and by 1807, Monroe had returned to the United States. He served one term in the Virginia legislature in 1810 and was elected to another term as Virginia governor in 1811 but left in order to join the Madison administration in Washington, D.C.

Our Fifth President

James Madison was inaugurated president of the United States in 1809. He was unhappy with his first secretary of state, and in early 1811, Madison asked James Monroe to step into the position. Monroe served as Madison's secretary of state for the rest of Madison's two terms. Monroe also stepped in to serve as secretary of war during the War of 1812, serving in both positions at the same time for a while. Both positions made use of the skills Monroe had developed during the American Revolution and during his time as a diplomat abroad. By the time of the 1816 presidential election, Monroe was the heir apparent for the Republican nomination.

By 1816, the Federalist Party had largely fallen into disarray and failed to present much competition for the election. Monroe easily won and was inaugurated the fifth president of the United States in 1817.

The two terms of James Monroe's presidency would later become known as the "Era of Good Feelings," a period of relative peace and economic growth after years of war. Monroe took time to travel across the country on a goodwill tour and spent thousands of dollars restoring the White House and other buildings that had been damaged by the British during the War of 1812. He was so popular that he ran unopposed for his second term and was easily reelected in 1820 with 231 out of 232 electoral votes. (One elector voted against Monroe to preserve George Washington's status as the only president elected unanimously.)

Missouri Compromise and Monroe Doctrine

James Monroe's presidency is best known for two things: the Missouri Compromise and the Monroe Doctrine. Both are indicative of the two things that Monroe was most concerned about during his presidency: westward expansion and national security. The Louisiana Purchase and the War of 1812, both of which Monroe had an important role in, firmly established the United States' hold on North American land and political status in relation to European powers. Once those issues had been settled, Monroe

The Monroe House in Washington, D.C., where James Monroe lived while serving as secretary of state. *Photograph by Camille Dierksheide.*

was able to focus on incorporating the new territories into the United States and solidifying the national borders.

Monroe believed that the new territories should be organized into states and admitted into the union as soon as possible. A total of five states joined the United States during his presidency: Mississippi, Illinois, Alabama, Maine and Missouri. Monroe also succeeded in purchasing Florida from Spain in 1819, allowing for its eventual entry into the union as well.

Monroe's state creation goals were not without controversy, however. They hit a bump in 1819, when Missouri applied to join the union. Until that point, it was generally believed that a new state could choose whether to allow slavery by writing it into its state constitution. In this case, Missouri wanted to allow slavery. But northern Congressmen objected to the addition of a new slave state into the United States, arguing that it was time to stop the expansion of slavery in the country. Southern slaveowners argued that Congress had no right to restrict slavery. After several months of debate in Congress, Monroe signed the Missouri Compromise in March 1820. Missouri would be admitted as a slave state, Maine as a free state and slavery would be prohibited north of the 36°30′line in the Louisiana Purchase.

In the early 1820s, several countries in South America began to revolt against Spanish rule. Beginning in 1822, Monroe indicated his support of the fledgling nations by granting them diplomatic recognition. During Monroe's Christmas address to Congress in 1823, he declared that European nations should consider the Western Hemisphere closed to future colonization and that any effort of a European power to extend monarchy to the western hemisphere would be considered a hostile act by the United States. This was directed at both Spain and Russia, which was making incursions into northern Canada. In addition, Monroe stated that the United States would remain neutral and uninvolved in European political affairs and wars. Although this statement had no real standing in international law, it became known as the Monroe Doctrine and became a foundation of U.S. international relations for many years.

Views on Slavery

Over the course of his life, James Monroe owned four plantations and at least seventy enslaved people, who labored on those plantations. He had been raised in a home with enslaved staff and inherited the ownership of those people upon his father's death in 1774. He owned enslaved people throughout his life, and they worked on all his plantations and in the White House. In

1810, there were forty-nine enslaved people living at his plantation, Highland, near Charlottesville, Virginia. Currently, two independent researchers are compiling information on the enslaved people who lived at Highland and what became of them and their descendants.

Although Monroe spoke about the necessity of eventually abolishing slavery, he was most concerned about preserving the union and was unwilling to challenge his fellow southern slave owners whose wealth was tied up in the plantation economy and the enslaved people who supported it. He was also among the group of elites who believed that formerly enslaved people should not live in the United States and supported the efforts of the American Colonization Society to create a colony in western Africa for freed people.

Ultimately, Monroe's political career was largely dependent on the money that was earned for him by enslaved laborers on his tobacco plantations, and he was unwilling to give that up. By 1823, he owned between sixty and seventy people on his plantations. Upon his death, he freed just one person, his enslaved manservant Peter Marks.

Retirement

After leaving the White House, James and Elizabeth Monroe retired to Oak Hill, their plantation in Louden County, Virginia. Monroe ventured back into politics briefly and participated in the Virginia Constitutional Convention in 1829. The following year, Elizabeth died. James sold Oak Hill and moved in with his daughter Maria and her family in New York City. James Monroe died of tuberculosis and heart failure the following year, on July 4, 1831, the third founding father to die on Independence Day. He was originally buried in New York City's Marble Cemetery but, in 1858, was reinterred in an elaborate tomb in Hollywood Cemetery in Richmond, Virginia.

JAMES MONROE HISTORIC SITES IN VIRGINIA

JAMES MONROE BIRTHPLACE PARK AND MUSEUM
4460 James Monroe Highway, Colonial Beach, VA
540-603-6675
monroefoundation.org

James Monroe was born and raised in a modest house at this location on April 28, 1758. It originally comprised about five hundred acres, including an apple and peach orchard. James inherited the property upon the death of his father in 1774 and sold it six years later.

By the late 1800s, the Monroe birthplace no longer existed, but a circa-1845 engraving of the building survived. A 1976 archaeological survey identified the location of the house, and construction of a reproduction of the building on the original foundation began in 2017. The reproduction house, comprised of a parlor, dining room and upstairs bedrooms, is now complete, and the James Monroe Memorial Foundation is working to furnish it with period pieces and reproductions. The foundation is also working to restore a historical Black cemetery on the grounds.

The site now comprises seventy-four acres, a visitor center and a walking trail. Free guided tours of the reproduction house are offered on Saturdays and Sundays during the summer.

A modern reconstruction of the house where James Monroe was born at the James Monroe Birthplace Park and Museum. *Courtesy of the James Monroe Memorial Foundation.*

HIGHLAND

2050 James Monroe Parkway, Charlottesville, VA
434-293-8000
highland.org

In 1793, James Monroe purchased one thousand acres of land outside of Charlottesville, Virginia, near the home of his friend and colleague Thomas Jefferson. Construction on a house began in 1797, and the Monroes moved into the house in 1799. A guest house was added to the grounds in 1818. For the next two decades, the Monroes spent most of their time in either Richmond or Washington as they followed James's political career. They would return sporadically to Highland for vacations and holidays. In the interim, the plantation was managed by a series of overseers, and about fifty enslaved workers labored on the farm and in the tobacco fields.

In 1826, after leaving the White House, Monroe sold his Highland plantation and the enslaved people who worked and lived there. Shortly after the sale, the main house on the plantation was burned to the ground. The plantation passed through several hands over the next century, and in 1974, it was given to the College of William and Mary. At some point over the decades, a story began to be told that the 1818 guest house, which is still standing, was part of the original house lived in by the Monroes. For years, visitors would come to Highland and tour the guest house, believing it to be a wing of the Monroes' original home.

In 2012, Highland administrators launched an archaeological examination that eventually revealed that the site had been misinterpreted for many years. In 2016, the museum announced its discovery of the foundation of the original Monroe-era home and that the 1818 guest house was a separate structure. In 2020, during a forced closure due to the COVID-19 pandemic, staff revised the interpretation and exhibits to reflect the new discoveries.

Highland is currently comprised of the 1818 presidential guesthouse, an adjoining 1870s farmhouse and a portion of the original plantation. Self-guided exhibits inside the buildings talk about Monroe's life, the history of the grounds and the changing interpretations. Two rooms are set up as an early nineteenth-century guest house and feature furniture and objects that belonged to the Monroe family. The foundation of the original 1799 house that was lived in by the Monroes is marked by fieldstone and interpretive panels. There are also original and reconstructed outbuildings with exhibits about the enslaved people who lived and worked there.

The house and grounds are open daily for self-guided tours.

OAK HILL PLANTATION
Louden County, VA
nps.gov/places/oak-hill.htm

James Monroe inherited this property from his uncle in 1808 and eventually retired here after his two terms as president. The house was built between 1820 and 1823, and the plantation originally comprised two thousand acres. In addition to the Monroes, about fifty enslaved people lived and worked at Oak Hill. The house was sold out of the Monroe family in the late 1800s.

Oak Hill is privately owned and not open to the public.

JAMES MONROE MUSEUM AND MEMORIAL LIBRARY
908 Charles Street, Fredericksburg, VA
540-654-1043
jamesmonroemuseum.umw.edu

The James Monroe Museum was founded by a great-granddaughter of Monroe in a building that was originally believed to have been James's law office from 1786 to 1788. Rose de Chine Gouverneur Hoes opened the museum as the James Monroe Law Office Shrine in 1927, and her son Laurence Gouverneur spent decades collecting Monroe-related artifacts and archives. The museum and archives were given to the Commonwealth of Virginia in 1964, and the museum is currently operated by the University of Mary Washington. It was eventually discovered that the museum building was not Monroe's original law office, although Monroe did own the property.

The James Monroe Museum and Memorial Library in Fredericksburg. *Courtesy of the James Monroe Museum and Memorial Library.*

James Monroe's tomb in Richmond's Hollywood Cemetery. *Author's photograph.*

The museum currently interprets James Monroe's life and includes exhibits about his military service and time in the White House. Its artifacts include furniture that was used by the Monroes, including a Louis XVI secretary that is believed to be the desk on which Monroe wrote the Monroe Doctrine. Also on display are a dress worn by Elizabeth and suit worn by James.

The museum is open daily, and the exhibits are self-guided.

HOLLYWOOD CEMETERY

412 South Cherry Street, Richmond, VA
804-648-8501
hollywoodcemetery.org

James Monroe was buried in Hollywood Cemetery in Richmond. There is a map at the entrance to the cemetery that indicates the location of Monroe's grave in the Presidents' Circle. The cemetery is open daily.

OUTSIDE OF VIRGINIA

THE MONROE HOUSE

2017 I (Eye) Street Northwest, Washington, D.C.
202-331-7282
artsclubofwashington.org

The Monroe family lived in this townhouse around 1811, while James Monroe was serving as James Madison's secretary of state. The building is currently owned by the Arts Club of Washington, D.C., and is operated as an events venue. Exhibits in the house are open to the public.

5

WILLIAM HENRY HARRISON

Our Ninth President

Fast Facts About William Henry Harrison

- Ninth president of the United States.
- Born February 9, 1773; died April 4, 1841.
- Served for one month.
- Married Anna Symmes (1775–1864) in 1795.
- Children: Elizabeth Bassett (1796–1846), John Cleves Symmes (1798–1830), Lucy Singleton (1800–1826), William Henry (1802–1838), John Scott (1804–1878), Benjamin (1806–1840), Mary Symmes (1809–1842), Carter Bassett (1811–1839), Anna Tuthill (1813–1865) and James Findlay (1814–1817).
- Nicknamed "Old Tippecanoe."
- Served the shortest term in presidential history.
- The first president to die in office.
- The last president to be born a British subject.
- Prior careers: military officer, state legislator, senator, diplomat and county clerk.

William Henry Harrison, the ninth president of the United States. *Library of Congress, Prints and Photographs Division.*

ALL ABOUT WILLIAM HENRY HARRISON

The ninth president of the United States, William Henry Harrison, is generally ranked at the bottom of lists of the nation's best presidents. But in all fairness, he barely had time to unpack his suitcases in the White House before he was dead. Harrison was the first president to die while in office and served the shortest presidential term, just thirty-one days. Yet he had a long military and political career in the northwestern United States prior to his nomination and was an immensely popular candidate, so it is interesting to speculate what influence he might have had on American politics had he survived longer than a month in office.

Early Life

William Henry Harrison was born on February 9, 1773, to Elizabeth Harrison and her husband, Benjamin Harrison V, at Berkeley Plantation, a one-thousand-acre plantation on the banks of the James River in what is now rural Charles City, Virginia. The Harrisons were part of colonial Virginia aristocracy, tracing their roots back to Benjamin Harrison I, who arrived in the colony of Jamestown in 1633. William was the youngest of the eight Harrison children and enjoyed a comfortable childhood of wealth and privilege on an estate that was served by as many as one hundred enslaved workers.

William was just two years old when the American Revolution began. His father, Benjamin Harrison V, spent long stretches away from home, serving in the Continental Congress in Philadelphia and in Richmond as a member of the Virginia legislature and then as Virginia's governor. Although they lived not far from some of the Revolution's battle sites, the Harrisons were largely protected from the effects of war—with one exception. In 1781, the Harrisons were forced to leave Berkeley Plantation to go into hiding for a month while the British, led by traitor Benedict Arnold, ransacked their house.

William was tutored at home until the age of fourteen, at which time he enrolled at Hampden-Sydney College, located southwest of Richmond in rural Virginia. William aspired to become a medical doctor and studied at Hampden-Sydney for three years. He then moved first to Richmond to study

Berkeley Plantation, the home of William Henry Harrison. *Photograph by Gary Smith Images and courtesy of Berkeley Plantation.*

under a local doctor and then to the University of Pennsylvania Medical School in Philadelphia. But shortly after his arrival in Philadelphia in 1791, William received word that his father had died. Following the customs of the time, the Harrisons' eldest son inherited Berkeley Plantation and his father's estate. His income cut off, eighteen-year-old William reevaluated his career plans and obtained a commission into the army.

Military Career

William Henry Harrison joined the First American Regiment as an ensign and was sent west to help force Native Americans out of the newly acquired Northwest Territory in order to clear land for white settlement. Harrison would spend the bulk of his military and political career in these new territories, only returning east for his brief tenure in the White House.

The Northwest Territory, a chunk of land comprising present-day Ohio, Indiana, Michigan, Illinois and a part of Minnesota, was won by the United States from Great Britain during the American Revolution. Although the 1783 Treaty of Paris transferred the ownership of this land to the United States, the resident British were slow to depart, and negotiations did not include the people who had been living on the contested land for generations: members of the Shawnee, Lenape, Miami and other Native American tribes. The new United States government embarked on a two-pronged path to shore up its territorial claims, encouraging occupation of the land by white settlers while clearing indigenous people off the land by either negotiation or force.

In the fall of 1791, Harrison was sent west to Fort Washington, near today's Cincinnati, Ohio, to help defend the new territory. He served under General Anthony Wayne at the Battle of Fallen Timbers in 1794; there, the U.S. Army defeated a coalition of Native American tribes, forcing them to sign over most of the land that comprises today's Ohio. Harrison distinguished himself as a competent soldier during the battle and was made commander.

Shortly after his move to the Northwest Territory, Harrison met Anna Tuthill Symmes, the daughter of a local farmer and judge. In 1795, the couple married in secret, against Anna's father's wishes (but he would eventually come around). Harrison purchased a 160-acre farm in North Bend on the Ohio River and moved his young family there. The Harrisons would eventually have a total of ten children, the youngest of whom died in early childhood.

Governor of Indiana Territory

In 1798, Harrison left the army and, at the bequest of his father-in-law, received an appointment as secretary of the Northwest Territory. The following year, Harrison was elected to represent the Northwest Territory in Congress. It was a nonvoting position but gave Harrison a voice in Congress to encourage policies that would expand settlement in the Northwest Territories, with the aim of eventual statehood for the region. Harrison promoted the Land Act of 1800, which reduced the size of a piece of property that could be purchased to 320 acres (at two dollars per acre), which made land ownership possible for more settlers. Harrison also urged splitting the Northwest Territory in half; he was appointed the first governor of the Territory of Indiana, a position he held from 1801 to 1812. During that time, he moved his family to the capital, Vincennes, and built his family a brick mansion that he named Grouseland.

As governor of the Territory of Indiana, Harrison's main job was to acquire land from Native American tribes and expand white settlement so that Indiana could eventually obtain statehood. During his tenure as governor, Harrison persuaded Native American tribes to give up fifty million acres of land in often-questionable treaties and at a cost of less than two cents per acre. These treaties were not without controversy and consequences, however, as Native American leaders fought back against white encroachment on their land.

Battle of Tippecanoe

William Henry Harrison obtained his nickname "Old Tippecanoe" from a battle that he fought against the Shawnee, who refused to give up their land to the U.S. government. In 1809, Harrison negotiated the purchase of nearly thirty million acres of land in what is now southeastern Indiana in the Treaty of Fort Wayne. Harrison negotiated the purchase from a group of Potawatomie, Lenape and Miami chiefs but ignored the Shawnee tribe who also lived on the land and did not want to sell. Shawnee chief Tecumseh argued that the treaty was invalid, because all Native American land was owned in common by all tribes, and he began building a pan-tribal confederacy to oppose the Americans.

In November 1811, Harrison led a group of soldiers north from Vincennes, Indiana, to build a new fort near the Shawnee village of

Prophetstown, where Tecumseh's brother lived. The Shawnee, concerned that the Americans were going to attack, made a preemptive strike on the soldiers. Harrison's soldiers counterattacked and burned Prophetstown to the ground. This battle became known as the Battle of Tippecanoe, and Harrison was celebrated for his leadership with a nickname from the battle.

In June 1812, the United States declared war on Great Britain, largely over its interference with American ships and the blockade of trade. In the territories, however, the War of 1812 was more focused on fighting Native American tribes who had allied with the British, including Tecumseh's confederacy of Native American tribes. At the declaration of war, Harrison rejoined the army and was appointed general, with command over the Army of the Northwest. In October 1913, he led 5,000 soldiers against a British and indigenous force of 1,700 in the Battle of Thames in Canada. During the battle, Tecumseh was killed. With Tecumseh's death, his alliance of Native American tribes faltered and then fell apart. Harrison was celebrated as a hero.

Road to the White House

After the War of 1812, forty-one-year-old Harrison retired from the army and moved his family back to their home in North Bend, Ohio. He also returned to his political career. He served as a member of the U.S. House of Representatives from 1816 to 1819, then in the Ohio State Senate from 1819 to 1821. (His property straddled the Indiana-Ohio border, so he was able to serve in both states.) He was elected to the U.S. Senate from Ohio in 1825 and was appointed envoy to Colombia for a year in 1828.

Although Harrison's post-military career may appear to have been a straight climb up the political ladder, it was not. He made frequent attempts to launch business ventures, none of them particularly successful, and spent the years between 1836 and 1840 in the rather unglamorous position of county court clerk in Cincinnati, Ohio. The reality was that he was constantly struggling to bring in enough income to support his large family at anywhere near the standard of living he had as a child in Virginia. In addition to their ten children, the Harrisons also took in at least two orphaned children and, in the 1830s, found themselves supporting grandchildren as well. Harrison was described by his contemporaries as generous and entertaining, someone who always had an extra seat at his dining room table. Unfortunately, he struggled to afford that lifestyle.

A drawing from William Henry Harrison's 1840 "log cabin" presidential campaign. In front of a log cabin, a shirtsleeved Harrison welcomes a soldier, inviting him to rest and partake of a barrel of "hard cider." Nearby, another soldier, already seated, drinks a glass of cider. On a staff to the right is an American flag emblazoned with "Harrison & Tyler." *Library of Congress, Prints and Photographs Division.*

In 1836, Harrison entered the running for the presidency at the behest of the Whig Party that was determined to defeat the Democrats. Their strategy was an inventive one; they selected three candidates from three different parts of the country—Daniel Webster from Massachusetts, Hugh Lawson White from Tennessee and Harrison from Ohio—and ran them all against the Democratic Party's candidate Martin Van Buren. Their goal was to prevent Van Buren from getting a majority of votes so that the election would have to be settled by the House of Representatives. The Whigs' plan failed; Van Buren won a majority of votes. But Harrison came in second.

The Whig Party tried again in 1840, this time launching what would become known as the first modern political campaign. The Democratic Party, running Van Buren for a second term, criticized Harrison's age (sixty-seven) and described him as a country farmer who would be better off drinking hard cider on the front porch of his log cabin. The Whigs embraced the criticism and celebrated Harrison as encompassing the best of humble frontier values. Harrison was championed as a war hero, an enterprising frontiersman and a humble farmer, while Van Buren was described as being out of touch with the common man. The Whigs rolled out the propaganda and launched everything from songs to soap celebrating Harrison's humble roots. A Philadelphia distiller, E.G. Booze, packaged whiskey in log cabin–shaped bottles, and the party gave them out as souvenirs. Prior to this time, it was generally considered unprofessional for a candidate for public office to participate in his own campaign, but Harrison spent the last weeks of the campaign on the road. A record 80 percent of eligible voters turned out for the election, and Harrison won.

Views on Slavery

Of course, none of the people who voted William Henry Harrison into the White House were women, Native Americans or people of color. Some states still required voters to own property, thus eliminating most immigrants from the voter rolls as well. Despite his "modern" presidential campaign, Harrison was very much a man of his times. He believed in Manifest Destiny—the idea that the United States had the God-given right and responsibility to expand to the Pacific Ocean—and that indigenous people should be forced off their ancestral lands in order to make way for that expansion.

Harrison was also an unapologetic enslaver. He was raised in a home with enslaved staff and likely took an enslaved manservant with him to college. The oral histories of the family of civil rights activist and NAACP secretary Walter Francis White (1893–1955) allege that Harrison fathered White's maternal grandmother and five other children with an enslaved woman named Dilsia.

Slavery was prohibited in the Northwest Territory but continued anyway. While governor, Harrison tried to persuade Congress to overturn the ban on

A reconstructed slave dwelling on the grounds of Berkeley Plantation. *Author's photograph.*

slavery. When that was unsuccessful, he just ignored it, choosing to interpret the law to mean that slaves couldn't be bought or sold in the territory but that owners could still bring slaves into the territory with them. In some cases, Harrison and other slaveowners in the territory converted their enslaved workers into indentured servants, and some may have eventually been freed from that status. While campaigning for president, he changed his politics from day to day, claiming to be both pro- and antislavery, depending on the audience. He was never held accountable for these contradictions, as he served as president for just thirty-one days.

Our Ninth President

On March 4, 1841—a cold, wet day in Washington, D.C.—William Henry Harrison delivered what would come to be the longest inaugural address in U.S. history at nearly two hours long. He committed to nothing in his

Presidential Inauguration of William Henry Harrison on March 4, 1841. Harrison became ill after his inauguration and died a month later. *Library of Congress, Prints and Photographs Division.*

speech, except that he would serve just one term and that he believed strongly in states' rights. Both before and after his inauguration, Harrison was overwhelmed by visitors and people who were seeking jobs and appointments in his government. He tried to see as many people as possible but was likely exhausted even before he took office.

On March 27, he was diagnosed with pneumonia and received the most advanced medical treatment available: bleeding, cupping and a regimen of pills. Despite his doctors' efforts, Harrison died on April 4, 1841.

Harrison was buried on family land in North Bend, Ohio. In the few years after his death, his three remaining daughters also died. His sole surviving child was the father of Benjamin Harrison (1833–1901), who eventually became the twenty-third president of the United States.

WILLIAM HENRY HARRISON HISTORIC SITES IN VIRGINIA

BERKELEY PLANTATION

12602 Harrison Landing Road, Charles City, VA
804-829-6018
berkeleyplantation.com

The Harrison family traces their roots at Berkeley Plantation to Benjamin Harrison IV, the grandfather of William Henry Harrison, who built the current manor house there in 1726. But the modern interpretation of the estate focuses less on the Harrisons and more on the other historical events that took place on the plantation. In fact, William Henry Harrison only gets a passing mention in the guided tour.

First up is Berkeley Plantation's claim that it is the home of the first Thanksgiving in America. Its argument: in December 1619, a group of thirty-eight white settlers disembarked from their ship onto the land that would eventually become Berkeley Plantation. As instructed by their captain, they immediately fell to their knees and "gave thanksgiving" for their safe arrival. This was, indeed, almost two years before the mythological "Pilgrims and Indians" celebration that most Americans learn about in kindergarten—which was, in turn, likely part of an annual harvest celebration held by the Wampanoag for generations. If you wish to argue the historical accuracy of this "first Thanksgiving" with your

A family on a tour of the interior of Berkeley Plantation. *Courtesy of Berkeley Plantation.*

tour guide, they will point you to a framed letter written by Massachusetts native and president John F. Kennedy, acknowledging Berkeley Plantation as the home of the first Thanksgiving.

Berkeley Plantation's second claim to fame is that it is the first place where bourbon whiskey was distilled in the New World, allegedly by George Thorpe, in 1620. There are several other families who stake their claim as being the first, but if we can assume that the distilling skills were brought over with the earlier white settlers, then there certainly weren't many who arrived before Thorpe. However, Thorpe and the other settlers did not last long at Berkeley Plantation. According to Berkeley Plantation interpreters, the original settlers were killed by Native Americans in 1622. The history of the plantation next picks up in 1691, when William Henry Harrison's ancestor built a shipyard at what is known as Harrison's Landing. In 1726, the present manor house was built by the Harrison patriarch and named Berkeley Plantation.

The guided tour of the house encompasses four rooms on the first floor; the second floor is the private quarters for the Jamison family, who purchased the plantation in 1907. Although the house had fallen into disrepair by the turn of the century and had apparently been used as a barn for a while, much of the house is original. Later, the plantation was occupied by General George McClellan's troops during the Civil War and served as both a prison for Union soldiers (note the bars on the basement windows) and a hospital for Confederate soldiers. (Make sure your tour guide shows you the hole in the floor where surgeons allegedly dumped amputated limbs into the basement, as it was bad for the soldiers' morale to let them pile up in the yard.)

The third claim to fame of Berkeley Plantation also dates to the Civil War: it was the location where the song "Taps" was written. The original bugle on which the song was played is part of the museum's collection and on display in the basement of the manor house.

The story of the enslaved people at Berkeley Plantation can be glimpsed here and there throughout the plantation. The kitchen dependency, a separate building, was connected to the main house by an underground tunnel so that the enslaved laborers' presence could be minimized; in the re-created slave cabins, which were built for the filming of a movie at the estate, there is an exhibit that displays the bills of sale for several of the Harrison' slaves; and the one thousand acres of the still-working plantation is now tended with modern farming equipment rather than the backbreaking labor of the enslaved.

Guided tours of the house are offered daily. The grounds and gardens are self-guided.

Outside of Virginia

William Henry Harrison's Grouseland

3 West Scott Street, Vincennes, IN
812-882-2096
grouseland.org

Grouseland was the home that William Henry Harrison built for his family in Vincennes, Indiana, while he was serving as governor of the Indiana Territory. The two-and-a-half story brick house has twenty-six rooms and thirteen fireplaces. The house is open daily for guided tours.

William Henry Harrison Tomb Historic Site

41 Cliff Road, North Bend, OH
844-288-7709
ohiohistory.org/visit/browse-historical-sites/william-henry-harrison-tomb

William Henry Harrison was buried on his family's estate in North Bend, Ohio. When the estate was sold, the ownership of the burial ground passed to the State of Ohio. Harrison was buried here, along with his wife and other members of the family. The site is open daily.

Harrison-Symmes Memorial Museum

112 South Miami Avenue, Cleves, OH
hsmfmuseum.org

This small museum interprets the life of William Henry Harrison and his father-in-law, John Cleves Symms. The museum is volunteer-run and only open by appointment, which can be requested on its website.

6

JOHN TYLER

Our Tenth President

- Tenth president of the United States.
- Born March 29, 1790, died January 18, 1862.
- Served one term: 1841–45.
- Married Letitia Christian (1790–1842) in 1813. Married Julia Gardiner (1820–1889) in 1844.
- Children with Letitia: Mary (1815–1847), Robert (1816–1877), John (1819–1896), Letitia (1821–1907), Elizabeth (1823–1850), Anne (1825–1825), Alice (1827–1854) and Tazewell (1830–1874). With Julia: David (1846–1927), John Alexander (1848–1883), Julia (1849–1871), Lachlan (1851–1902), Lyon (1853–1935), Robert Fitzwalter (1856–1927) and Margaret Pearl (1860–1947).
- The first vice president to take office after the death of a president.
- The first president to marry while in office.
- The only former president to defect to a foreign country.
- Fathered more children than any other president.
- Prior careers: planter, lawyer, state legislator, congressman and vice president.

John Tyler, the tenth president of the United States. *Library of Congress, Prints and Photographs Division.*

ALL ABOUT JOHN TYLER

John Tyler likely never expected to become president of the United States but fully embraced the role after the untimely death of his predecessor, William Henry Harrison. Yet even as president—the highest federal office in the land—Tyler continued to advocate for states' rights and independence over the federal government. And in the end, it was clear that his loyalties lay with his home state of Virginia, as he joined in secession from the Union upon the outbreak of the Civil War, making Tyler the first and only U.S. president to defect to a foreign country.

Early Life

John Tyler was born into a wealthy Virginia plantation family and grew up just down the street from William Henry Harrison, whom he would briefly serve under as vice president of the United States. John was the sixth of eight children born to Mary Marot Armistead Tyler and her husband, John Tyler Sr., a federal and state judge (and the former college roommate of Thomas Jefferson). The Tylers owned Greenway, a twelve-thousand-acre wheat, corn and tobacco plantation on the banks of the James River in Charles City County, Virginia, served by an estimated forty-five enslaved staff.

John was born on March 29, 1790, and was just seven years old when his mother died of a stroke. His father never remarried and was often absent, tending to his business and political interests, so Tyler was raised largely by his older sister Martha and a live-in housekeeper. John was an anxious child, prone to an upset stomach, but enjoyed the materially comfortable childhood of children of his class. He was tutored at home until he was old enough to enroll in the College of William and Mary in 1802. Upon his graduation, John went to live with his father in Richmond, where the senior Tyler had recently been elected governor of Virginia. John studied law for two years and was admitted to the bar in 1809. Like his father, however, the younger Tyler quickly found his interests lay in politics.

Political Career

In 1811, at the age of twenty-one, John Tyler was elected to the Virginia House of Delegates, where he served five one-year terms. It was there that he met Letitia Christian, the daughter of a fellow Virginia plantation owner. The couple fell in love and married on March 29, 1813, Tyler's twenty-third birthday. The couple built a home next to Tyler's family in Charles City County and named the estate Woodburn; eventually, they would purchase Tyler's childhood home as well.

In 1816, Tyler was elected to the U.S. House of Representatives, where he served until 1821. Letitia remained at home, managing their enslaved staff and raising their eight children, while Tyler's rising political career took him to Richmond, Williamsburg and Washington, D.C., for much of the year.

Over the course of his political career, Tyler would variously identify himself as a member of the Democratic-Republican, Democratic, Whig and "New" Democratic-Republican Parties—although he was never a stickler for ideology and was ostracized by two of these parties during his career. His beliefs were largely representative of his race, birthplace and social class as a white, Virginian, wealthy planter. Tyler's vision of the United States was that of a loose union of individual states with a weak federal government. He

A map of the United States in 1842. *Library of Congress, Geography and Map Division.*

came from a family with a long history of slave ownership and believed that the institution of slavery was a necessary evil. He was an ardent supporter of states' rights and opposed such things as federal spending on public works, protective tariffs (arguing that they would reduce southern exports) and the development of a national banking system. Unlike many of his southern peers, however, Tyler believed in what would come to be known as Manifest Destiny, the importance and inevitability of the United States' expansion to the Pacific Ocean. Each of these beliefs would be challenged during Tyler's time in office.

Historically, banks operated under state charters, meaning they could only open branches within a single state. In 1819, the Second National Bank, created just three years prior over the objection of many Southern Democrats, ran into financial trouble. During his term in the House of Representatives, Tyler was part of a congressional investigation into the bank's finances. Tyler, along with other Southern Democrats, objected to a national banking system, believing that it was an overreach of federal power and that each state should be responsible for its own debts and public projects. Tyler was hoping to be able to use the congressional investigation as a reason to revoke the charter of the Second National Bank but was unsuccessful in persuading Congress to join his cause. The national banking issue would again arise when Tyler ascended to the presidency.

A second issue that challenged Tyler was the debate that flourished in 1820 about whether to admit Missouri into the union as a slave or free state. Northern Republicans wanted to stop the spread of slavery completely. Southern Democrats, including Tyler, argued that it should be up to the individual states to decide whether to allow slavery. In the end, Congress reached what became known as the Missouri Compromise; Missouri would be admitted as a slave state, Maine would be admitted as a free state and there would be a line drawn at the 36°30′parallel, and no state north of that line would be permitted to have slavery.

In 1821, frustrated with his inability to get support for his ideas and suffering from gastrointestinal issues, Tyler left Congress and returned to his law practice. That lasted only two years until Tyler returned to politics with another two years in the Virginia House of Delegates (1823–25) and then two years as governor of Virginia (1825–27).

By 1827, Tyler was back in Washington, D.C., this time serving as a U.S. senator. There were several issues facing Congress, but many of them boiled down to the question of which entity had the greatest power: the federal government or individual states. In 1832, the government of South

Carolina attempted to nullify a federal tariff, arguing that state laws took precedence over federal laws. The issue of the national banking system continued to simmer, reaching a boiling point when President Andrew Jackson withdrew all federal funds from the Second National Bank in hopes that the move would force the bank's collapse. Several senators, including Tyler, viewed Jackson's move as an overstep of power and wanted to formally reprimand Jackson for the move, but the Virginia legislature pressured Tyler to vote against censure. Rather than go against his conscience, Tyler resigned from the Senate.

In 1834, defectors from the Democratic Party who opposed Andrew Jackson formed a new political party, the Whig Party. The Whigs were generally supportive of protective tariffs, federal subsidies for infrastructure and a national bank but were in opposition to national expansion. They also wanted Congress to be more powerful than the president. In 1836, as the nation faced a financial downturn that was largely the result of Andrew Jackson's financial decisions, the Whig Party determined to oust Democrat Martin Van Buren from the presidency. Their plan was to run three candidates from three different parts of the country in hopes of splitting votes and making sure Van Buren couldn't get the majority needed to win outright. That would then throw the decision-making to the House of Representatives.

By then, Tyler had migrated to the Whig Party, and party leadership ran him as one of two vice presidential candidates. The party believed that Tyler would appeal to southerners who believed strongly in states' rights. The Whigs lost in 1836, but the 1840 ticket of "Tippecanoe and Tyler, Too" won. The role of vice president in the early nineteenth century was largely ceremonial, and Tyler likely expected that he could serve out his four years at home in Virginia. That lasted until April 4, 1841, when William Henry Harrison died just thirty-one days into his term as president.

Our Tenth President

Not until the passage of the Twenty-Fifth Amendment in 1965 was it specified exactly what should happen when a president dies in office. The Constitution says that in case of the death of the president, the office of the presidency shall "devolve" onto the vice president. But in 1841, there was debate as to whether that meant the vice president should just assume the presidential duties or whether he would actually become president. Tyler

TYLER RECEIVING THE NEWS OF HARRISON'S DEATH.

Tyler Receiving the News of Harrison's Death, 1841. Library of Congress, Prints and Photographs Division.

took matters into his own hands and insisted to Harrison's cabinet that he should be sworn in as president. He was.

The Whig Party believed that Congress should have more power than the president and had counted on Harrison to be something of a figurehead as president. Tyler was not interested in stepping into that role. Fairly quickly, Tyler went to war with Congress. Twice in May 1941, Congress proposed the charter of another national bank, and Tyler vetoed both. In September 1841, five out of six members of Tyler's cabinet resigned, and the Whig Party kicked him out of its ranks. As a result of his ongoing battles with Congress, Tyler was able to accomplish very little in the domestic arena during his presidency.

Tyler had far more success in the international arena, however. In 1842, his secretary of state negotiated a new boundary between Maine and Canada with Great Britain (the Webster-Ashburton Treaty). In December that year, Tyler interceded to stop Great Britain from having undue influence over Hawaii. In 1844, Tyler signed the United States' first treaty with China (the Treaty of Wanghia), opening the country for trade. And at the end of his term, Tyler successfully navigated international relations with Mexico in order to annex Texas as a state, greatly expanding the area of the United States.

On a personal front, on September 10, 1842, Tyler's wife, Letitia, died after being ill for most of their time in the White House. She had given birth to a total of eight children, and her health grew worse after each delivery. She likely suffered from high blood pressure and migraines and had suffered two strokes before her death. Less than two years later, Tyler remarried. His second wife, Julia Gardiner, was the wealthy socialite daughter of a New York Senator and was thirty years Tyler's junior. The two had met when the Gardiners visited the White House in February 1843, and John proposed to Julia just a few weeks later. The two were married on June 26, 1844. She spent the last few months of Tyler's presidency redecorating the White House, mostly using her own funds.

By 1844, Tyler returned to his Democratic Party roots and considered a run for that year's presidential election. In the end, however, he decided to use the last of his political cache to force the Democratic Party to support the annexation of Texas. Some background: In 1836, Texas declared its independence from Mexico and requested to join the United States. The United States, however, was concerned that recognizing Texas would jeopardize international relations with Mexico. Tyler spent time in secret negotiations with Texas, but as his term was nearing its end, it looked like he would not be able to pull off the deal. So, during the 1844 Democratic Convention, Tyler held his own third-party convention and promoted himself as a presidential candidate under banners reading "Tyler and Texas." He lured enough people away from the Democratic Party that the Democrats were forced to take a stand supporting the annexation of Texas. Tyler withdrew his candidacy and put his support behind the Democratic candidate James Polk, who ran against Whig candidate Henry Clay. Polk won, and in February 1845, Congress passed a resolution to annex Texas. Tyler signed the measure into law just three days before he left office.

Views on Slavery

John Tyler was an unapologetic advocate for the institution of chattel slavery and fought against any suggestion that slavery should be abolished in the United States. He owned several hundred enslaved people during his lifetime. Tyler was raised on a plantation that was completely dependent on the labor of at least forty enslaved agricultural laborers and house servants. Upon his father's death in 1813, Tyler inherited the ownership of thirteen enslaved people; his wife brought more into their marriage. He had enslaved staff working for him at the White House, a situation that visitors from northern states and foreign countries sometimes found disturbing. And when Tyler left the White House and retired to his Virginia plantation, Sherwood Forest, there were likely up to seventy enslaved workers under his authority.

Several times over the course of his political career, Tyler spoke about how he opposed the buying and selling of people, but in 1827, he sought to sell one of his family's favorite enslaved workers, a woman named Ann Eliza, in order to finance his room and board in Washington, D.C. In December 1841, an abolitionist newspaper editor accused Tyler of having impregnated an unnamed enslaved woman on his staff and of having sold some of those children. According to research compiled by Frances Tyler, there is at least one family in the Tidewater area of Virginia whose family tradition says they are descended from Tyler and an enslaved woman. John Tyler did not free any of his enslaved staff in his will.

Retirement

Upon leaving the White House, Tyler retired to a new home in Charles City County, Virginia, with his second wife. Tyler had sold Greenway and Woodburn and purchased another plantation on the James River, which

Members of the Tyler family and their horses on the north lawn of the family's estate, Sherwood Forest, in the 1970s. *Courtesy of Sherwood Forest.*

he named Sherwood Forest, as he considered himself an "outlaw" from both the Democrat and Whig Parties. The plantation was supported by an estimated forty enslaved staff. He and Julia had an additional seven children, whom they raised at Sherwood Forest.

Sixteen years after leaving office, Tyler was invited by President James Buchanan to preside over a peace conference, called in February 1861 to try to forestall the South's secession from the United States. It was not successful, and Tyler soon turned his support to the Confederacy, delivering a speech that called for Virginia to secede from the union. In April 1861, it did, and Tyler headed the commission that negotiated Virginia's admittance into the Confederate States of America.

With those actions, Tyler became the first (and only) former president to defect to a foreign country. The Tyler family became active supporters of the Confederacy (three sons and four grandsons served in the Confederate military). In November 1861, Tyler was appointed to a seat in the Confederate House of Representatives. In January 1862, he moved to Richmond but had a stroke before he was seated. He died on January 18, 1862. His death was commemorated in the Confederacy but largely ignored in Washington, D.C.

Tyler had hoped to be buried at Sherwood Forest, but due to the war, he ended up at Hollywood Cemetery in Richmond, Virginia.

JOHN TYLER HISTORIC SITES IN VIRGINIA

SHERWOOD FOREST

14501 John Tyler Memorial Highway, Charles City, VA
804-829-5377
sherwoodforest.org

Sherwood Forest is located along John Tyler Memorial Highway (also known as Route 5) in rural Charles City, Virginia. The house is still owned by the Tyler family. Amazingly, due to Tyler men marrying much younger second wives, John Tyler's grandson is still alive and lived in the house until a few years ago.

Sherwood Forest is the house that John and Julia Tyler retired to when they left the White House in 1845. The original house was built in 1730 and renovated by the Tylers in 1844. The Tylers bought what was then known as

Sherwood Forest, John Tyler's retirement estate, has remained in the Tyler family for more than 175 years. *Courtesy of Sherwood Forest.*

Walnut Grove from a cousin in 1841 and renamed it Sherwood Forest. The current "Big House" is three hundred feet long, making it the longest wood frame house in America. At the time of John and Julia Tyler's residency, the plantation comprised 1,600 acres; it now comprises 3,500 acres.

The grounds of Sherwood Forest are open daily for self-guided tours. A map of the grounds is available at a welcome kiosk, and the tour includes stops to view the outside of the Big House, "Servant's House," various dependencies (kitchen, milk house, smoke house, et cetera), formal gardens and Tyler's law office.

Tours of the Big House are available by appointment. The house tour visits four rooms of the first floor of the house—the dining room, drawing room, parlor and ballroom—which hold an eclectic assortment of antique and modern family pieces. The remainder of the house is still used by the Tyler family. Of particular interest is an eighteenth-century sideboard, which family lore says was owned by John Tyler and subsequently damaged during a house fire set by Union soldiers who occupied the plantation during the Civil War.

John Tyler's tombstone at Richmond's Hollywood Cemetery. *Author's photograph.*

A recent house tour was led by a Tyler family friend who was very knowledgeable about the history of the Tylers but generally overlooked the enslaved staff who built and supported the plantation. A Tyler descendant has researched and compiled information on several of the enslaved families who lived at Sherwood Forest, and staff report plans to incorporate that information into future tours.

GREENWAY PLANTATION
Route 5, Charles City, VA
37°20.371'N, 77°4.937'W

Greenway, the house where John Tyler was born, is marked with a historic sign about a mile west of Sherwood Forest. The house is privately owned and not open for tours.

HOLLYWOOD CEMETERY
412 South Cherry Street, Richmond, VA
804-648-8501
hollywoodcemetery.org

John Tyler was buried in Hollywood Cemetery in Richmond. There is a map at the entrance to the cemetery that indicates the location of Tyler's grave in the Presidents' Circle. The cemetery is open daily.

7

ZACHARY TAYLOR

Our Twelfth President

Fast Facts About Zachary Taylor

- Twelfth president of the United States.
- Born November 24, 1784; died July 9, 1850.
- Served for sixteen months.
- Married Margaret Mackall Smith (1788–1852) in 1810.
- Children: Ann Mackall (1811–1875), Sarah Knox (1814–1835), Octavia Pannell (1816–1820), Margaret Smith (1819–1820), Mary Elizabeth (1824–1909) and Richard (1826–1879).
- Nicknamed "Old Rough and Ready."
- The first president to be elected without having held any prior political office.
- The second president to die in office.
- The last president to own enslaved people while in office.
- The only person to receive three Congressional Gold Medals.
- Prior careers: military officer and planter.

All About Zachary Taylor

Zachary Taylor was a career army officer who rode his military victories in the Mexican-American War into the White House. He was born in Virginia,

A photograph of Zachary Taylor, the twelfth president of the United States, taken by Civil War photographer Mathew B. Brady. *Library of Congress, Prints and Photographs Division.*

raised in Kentucky and spent most of his life in military outposts on the frontiers of the rapidly expanding United States. He fought Native Americans in the north and west, Mexicans in the south and, while president, fought to hold the country together as the debate over slavery in the territories reached a fever pitch. One wonders if he might have been more successful if he hadn't died just sixteen months after taking office.

Early Life

If everything had gone according to plan, Zachary Taylor would have been born in Kentucky. His father, Richard Taylor, was a well-to-do Virginia planter who descended from *Mayflower* passengers and was a cousin of the father of future president James Madison. In 1783, as a bonus for his service in the war, the senior Taylor received a grant of one thousand acres of undeveloped land in what was then western Virginia. Having visited the Ohio River Valley as a young man and, perhaps, yearning for a bit more adventure and possibility, Richard sold his plantation and made plans to move his family west.

By the time the family departed in the fall of 1784, Richard's wife, Sarah Sabney Strother Taylor, was pregnant with their third child. The traveling party stopped for their first night at the home of a relative in Orange County, Virginia, where a member of their party fell ill. Richard continued on to Kentucky to clear land for a home, but the rest of the group ended up staying in Orange County for several months. It was there, on November 24, 1784, at a plantation named Montebello, that Sarah Taylor delivered her son Zachary.

Despite their rocky start, the Taylor family prospered in Kentucky. They first settled in a wooden cabin on Beargrass Creek, about five miles from what was then the small frontier town of Louisville. Soon thereafter, they were able to move into a more substantial brick home, which they named Springfield. Richard set about acquiring more property and the people to work the property. By 1800, he had expanded the plantation to 700 acres and owned another ten thousand acres of land across Kentucky. The Taylors also owned at least twenty-six enslaved people.

Zachary grew up surrounded by the wilderness of the Kentucky frontier alongside four brothers, three sisters and the enslaved men, women and children who labored at Springfield. He learned how to shoot, trap game and ride horses and likely had some interaction with the Shawnee and

Cherokee who hunted in the area. He was taught to read and write by tutors, but his formal education was only sporadic, and he never attended college.

Over the course of Zachary's childhood, the population of the Louisville area increased tenfold, Kentucky attained statehood and the United States added 828,000 square miles to its territory with the 1803 Louisiana Purchase. In fact, a teenaged Zachary may have heard news of the great expedition across the newly acquired lands that was being planned by Meriwether Lewis and William Clark, who organized and outfitted their trip nearby. Perhaps those stories inspired Zachary to seek his own adventures when, at the age of twenty-three, he enlisted in the U.S. Army.

Military Career

Zachary Taylor spent his forty-year military career defending the western and southern borders of the United States. He fought in the War of 1812, the Black Hawk War, the Second Seminole War and the Mexican-American War. He also spent long stretches of time in rudimentary accommodations on frontier outposts far from his family and where his only company were a dozen or two fellow servicemen and enslaved staff. Taylor was reportedly a

"A Little More Grape Capt. Bragg." General Zachary Taylor at the Battle of Buena Vista during the Mexican-American War. *Library of Congress, Prints and Photographs Division.*

competent leader who preferred an informal style of dress and conduct and was often found astride his favorite horse, Whitey.

As Taylor rose through the military ranks, he was deployed back and forth across the country. He spent his first few years in the army stationed in and around New Orleans. In July 1811, he was sent north to Indiana Territory, where he served under then-governor (and later president) William Henry Harrison and gained recognition for defending Fort Harrison from the attacks of Shawnee warriors at the start of the War of 1812. He returned to Kentucky for a bit and was then dispatched to St. Louis, Des Moines, Green Bay and then back to Kentucky. From 1822 to 1824, Taylor was back in Louisiana, this time as the commanding officer of Fort Robertson. He was then sent north to command troops who were fighting Native Americans in northwest Illinois during the Black Hawk War (1832). He was in Florida for the Second Seminole War (1835–1842), again fighting indigenous people who were resisting white settlement and forced relocation. On Christmas Day 1837, Taylor led his troops through waist-deep swamp muck in a successful attack against the Seminole in the Battle of Lake Okeechobee. This battle earned Taylor the nickname "Old Rough and Ready" and a promotion to general. Taylor remained in Florida until 1840, then went home for an extended leave to check on his plantations. He spent the next few years in Arkansas and Louisiana.

It was Taylor's military victories during the Mexican-American War (1846–1848) that brought him national fame and launched his political career. In 1845, the United States formally annexed Texas as the twenty-eighth state of the Union. However, there were lingering disputes over the location of the southern border of the state with Mexico. (The United States established the Rio Grande as the state's southern border; Mexico insisted it was farther north.) U.S. president James Polk wanted to buy the land between Texas and California (what would eventually become the American Southwest), but Mexico didn't want to sell.

By January 1846, Polk's diplomatic efforts had failed, and he was willing to go to war to defend the Texas border and force Mexico to part with the southwestern land. Polk ordered Taylor to the Rio Grande with instructions to not initiate hostilities but to respond as needed if the Mexicans attacked. Taylor set up his troops just north of the Rio Grande in disputed territory, and as predicted, Mexican troops attacked, and the U.S. Congress declared war. Taylor led his troops to victories at the Battles of Palo Alto and Resaca de la Palma, then continued south. Both sides suffered losses at the Battle of Monterrey, but Taylor was able to take the city. The largest battle of the war occurred the following February, when Taylor's greatly outnumbered troops bested Mexico at the Battle of Buena Vista, securing northern Mexico for the United States and the eventual victory in the Mexican-American War. Polk would get his land, and Taylor would get three Congressional Gold Medals for his service.

Family Life

The U.S. Army of the 1820s and 1830s recognized the hardships inherent with manning of frontier outposts and granted fairly long leaves of absence during peacetime. It was on one such leave, just one year into his career, that Zachary Taylor met the daughter of a wealthy Maryland tobacco planter who was in Kentucky to visit her married sister. In June 1810, after a short courtship, Taylor married Margaret Mackall Smith. Their first child was born the following year. The couple had a total of six children: five girls followed by a boy. It is unclear how often Peggy, as she was known, and the children followed Taylor to his postings, but they spent at least some time in Indiana Territory and Louisiana, as well as the Taylor family homestead at Springfield.

The Taylor children were raised Episcopalian, and their parents spared no expense to ensure their children had the education Zachary never had. Their son, Richard, traveled in Europe and graduated from Yale. The girls were also educated. However, only four of the children survived to adulthood. In the summer of 1820, while visiting family in Louisiana, Peggy and the children came down with malaria. Both three-year-old Octavia Pannell and infant Margaret Smith succumbed to the disease. Years later, the Taylors' second-born daughter, Sarah Knox, would also die of malaria, just three months after her wedding to Jefferson Davis (who would eventually remarry and lead the Confederate States during the Civil War).

As a wedding gift, Taylor's father gave Zachary and Margaret 324 acres of land near Springfield. Taylor sold the property shortly thereafter, turning him a tidy profit and launching the side businesses he would keep for the remainder of his life as a planter and land speculator. When he was stationed in Louisiana, he purchased a 380-acre sugar plantation north of Baton Rouge. In 1842, he bought a 2,000-acre cotton plantation on the Mississippi River. The purchase of Cypress Grove, as the plantation was known, included the purchase of eighty-one enslaved men, women and children. Although the Taylor family occasionally lived on their plantations, for the most part, they left them to be managed by white overseers, often a Taylor relative.

Views on Slavery

As president, Zachary Taylor advocated against the expansion of slavery into western territories while continuing to be an unapologetic enslaver himself. Taylor was raised on a plantation supported by the labor of enslaved staff. While serving in the northern territories that outlawed slavery, Taylor was among many southern slaveowners who ignored the laws and kept enslaved staff, even receiving extra payments from the military for their board. Over the course of his lifetime, Taylor owned more than 300 enslaved men, women and children, who worked on his plantations, in his homes and as personal servants on military outposts. Taylor brought an estimated 15 to 20 enslaved cooks, seamstresses, valets and maids with him when he entered the White House and willed the ownership of 131 enslaved people to his family members upon his death in 1850. Walt Bachman, the author of *The Last White House Slaves*, uncovered evidence that Taylor also fathered at least one child with an enslaved servant named Jane.

Our Twelfth President

The Whig Party began eyeing Taylor as a presidential candidate soon after his victory at the Battle of Buena Vista during the Mexican-American War. They hoped to replicate the success they'd had with another war hero, William Henry Harrison, in the 1840 election. Taylor had been largely apolitical up to that point and, in fact, had not previously voted in a presidential election. Eventually, though, he agreed to join the Whig Party, and in June 1848, he was nominated as the party's candidate for president. The Whigs selected Millard Fillmore as his running mate. The Democratic Party nominated Lewis Cass, and former Democratic president Martin Van Buren ran on an antislavery platform under the newly formed Free Soil Party ticket.

As it had in 1840, the Whig Party had no specific platform for the 1848 election—but neither did the competing parties. The Whigs did not replicate the showmanship of 1840, instead relying on Taylor's name recognition. The presidential election was held on November 7, 1848—the first time that all eligible voters went to the polls to vote for the president on the same date. Taylor won with 47 percent of the popular vote and 163 of the 290 electoral votes. He was the last Whig elected to office and the last southern president until Woodrow Wilson's election in 1912.

Congressional Scales: A True Balance. This political cartoon is a satire of Zachary Taylor's attempts to balance southern and northern interests on the question of slavery in 1850. Taylor stands on top of a pair of scales with a weight in each hand; the weight on the left reads "Wilmot Proviso," and the one on the right reads "Southern Rights." *Library of Congress, Prints and Photographs Division.*

When Taylor took office, one of the most important issues facing the federal government was the future of the territories that were acquired during the Mexican-American War. Under the 1848 Treaty of Guadalupe Hidalgo that ended the war, Mexico ceded 525,000 square miles of land to the United States. This land would eventually become the states of California, Nevada, Utah and portions of New Mexico and Arizona. But in 1848, northern and southern senators furiously debated whether the new territories would allow slavery or not. (Prior to their acquisition by the United States, the territories had operated under Mexican law, which banned slavery.) The South wanted the demarcation line at the 36°30′ parallel, which was decided on during the 1820 Missouri Compromise to indicate slave versus free states, to extend to the Pacific coast; the North wanted slavery banned in all new territories. For southerners, the debate was not just about slavery but power; they feared that if any of the new territories were admitted to the Union as free states (i.e., outlawing slavery), then the delicate balance of power in the Senate would shift, and there might be enough votes to outlaw slavery throughout the United States.

Complicating the matter was the flood of settlers who were making their way to the new territories. White settlers had been trekking west in covered wagons since the early 1840s, with an estimated one thousand migrants traveling the Oregon Trail in 1843 alone. In 1846, members of the Church of Latter-day Saints fled religious persecution in Illinois and settled in the area around the Great Salt Lake, increasing the population there. In January 1848, gold was discovered at Sutter's Mill, prompting the California Gold Rush (1848–55) and an influx of an estimated three hundred thousand forty-niners and followers before it died down. These people needed to be governed, represented and taxed.

The debate over slavery in the western territories grew increasingly bitter over the course of 1859. Southerners who expected Taylor to side with them were sorely disappointed when he announced that he believed that it was impractical to expand slavery into the western territories, arguing that the West had neither the landscape nor the climate to support a plantation economy. Several southern congressmen threatened to secede from the United States, prompting Taylor to say that he'd hang anyone who tried to disrupt the Union. Behind the scenes, Taylor encouraged Californians to bypass territorial status and petition Congress for statehood instead, allowing them to decide for themselves on the issue of slavery. They took the first step by drafting a state constitution in October 1849, a constitution that banned slavery. After Taylor's death, Congress passed the Compromise of 1850, which, in part, admitted California as a free state and enacted a stricter Fugitive Slave Act that required residents of free states to cooperate in the capture of escaped enslaved people. This compromise delayed conflict but did not resolve the issue of slavery in the United States.

Death

On July 4, 1850, Zachary Taylor attended an Independence Day celebration at the Washington Monument. It was a hot day, and afterward, he drank cold milk and ate a bowl of cherries. Sometime afterward, Taylor developed stomach cramps that progressed to a fever, severe vomiting and diarrhea over the next few days. It is unknown what made him ill, but Washington, D.C.'s water and sewage systems at the time were poor, and there were cholera outbreaks south of the city. Taylor was treated with opium, quinine, calomel (a mercury chloride) and bloodletting, none of which were successful. Taylor's last major act as president occurred on July 5, when he signed the Clayton-Bulwar Treaty with Great Britain, agreeing to not claim exclusive rights on a canal through Central America. Four days later, on July 9, 1850,

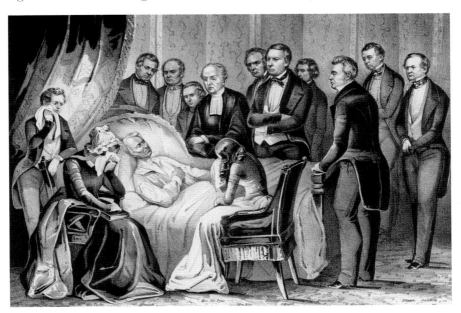

Death of General Z. Taylor. Zachary Taylor on his deathbed in 1850. *Library of Congress, Prints and Photographs Division.*

Taylor was dead. At the request of his wife, Taylor's body was returned to Kentucky for burial on family land.

Rumors about Taylor's death sprang up immediately. Some believed that he may have been assassinated. Eventually, in the 1980s, Taylor's body was exhumed and tested at Oak Ridge National Laboratory, a federal science center. No evidence of poisoning was found, and the laboratory confirmed the diagnosis of acute gastroenteritis, perhaps from contaminated food or drink.

ZACHARY TAYLOR HISTORIC SITES IN VIRGINIA

MONTEBELLO PLANTATION
38°9.234'N, 78°14.913'W
hmdb.org/m.asp?m=30181

The house where Zachary Taylor was born is no longer standing. A historic marker identifying the site is located at the intersection of Spotswood Trail (U.S. 33) and Old Montebello Drive near Gordonsville, Virginia. Please note that the house at this location is privately owned and is not the house where Taylor was born.

JAMES MADISON MUSEUM OF ORANGE COUNTY HERITAGE
129 Caroline Street, Orange, VA
540-672-1776
thejamesmadisonmuseum.net

This six-thousand-square-foot museum includes an eclectic collection of exhibits about the history of Orange County from prehistoric times through the nineteenth century. The museum is located in a former trucking business with a huge garage that currently holds a circa-1733 tenant house that was moved from another location in Orange County and an assortment of farm equipment and historic cars. The main hall features exhibits on the two presidents who were born in Orange County: James Madison and Zachary Taylor. Of particular interest are a bed, desk, clock and chair that were owned by Taylor. The museum is open daily and is self-guided.

Zachary Taylor's bed at the James Madison Museum. *Courtesy of the James Madison Museum of Orange County Heritage.*

OUTSIDE OF VIRGINIA

SPRINGFIELD PLANTATION

5608 Apache Road, Saint Matthews, KY

nps.gov/nr/travel/Presidents/zachary_taylor_springfield.html

The house where Zachary Taylor spent his childhood was once surrounded by a seven-hundred-acre plantation and the Kentucky wilderness. It is now privately owned and not open to the public.

ZACHARY TAYLOR NATIONAL CEMETERY

4701 Brownsboro Road, Louisville, KY

502-893-3852

cem.va.gov/CEMs/nchp/zacharytaylor.asp

The family mausoleum where Zachary Taylor was interred is now part of the Zachary Taylor National Cemetery. The cemetery is open daily.

Zachary Taylor National Cemetery in Louisville, Kentucky. *Photograph by Carol M. Highsmith and courtesy of the Library of Congress, Prints and Photographs Division.*

8

WOODROW WILSON

Our Twenty-Eighth President

FAST FACTS ABOUT WOODROW WILSON

- Twenty-Eighth president of the United States.
- Born December 28, 1856; died February 3, 1924.
- Served two terms: 1913–21.
- Married Ellen Louise Axson (1860–1914) in 1885 and Edith Bolling Galt (1872–1961) in 1915.
- Children with Ellen: Margaret Woodrow (1886–1944), Jessie Woodrow (1887–1933) and Eleanor Randolph (1889–1967).
- The only president to have earned a PhD.
- The last president to have lived in a home with enslaved staff.
- Awarded a Nobel Prize for founding the League of Nations.
- Prior careers: lawyer, professor, college president and governor.

ALL ABOUT WOODROW WILSON

More than sixty years passed between Zachary Taylor's death and the election of another Virginia-born president. In that time, the United States transformed both geographically and demographically, and Woodrow Wilson lived through many of those changes. He was born into a home with

Woodrow Wilson, the twenty-eighth president of the United States. *Library of Congress, Prints and Photographs Division.*

enslaved staff, lived through the Civil War and Reconstruction and came of age as the nation was transforming into a modern industrial society. He was elected to the presidency on a progressive agenda and succeeded in improving working conditions for small business owners and laborers. He saw the United States through the First World War and crafted a vision

The birthplace of Woodrow Wilson in Staunton. *Courtesy of the Woodrow Wilson Presidential Library and Museum.*

for an international peacekeeping organization that would eventually be realized after his death. Yet, despite these accomplishments, Wilson had a problematic track record when it came to racial equity during his time at Princeton University and in the White House. In that, he had something in common with his Virginian presidential predecessors.

Early Life

Thomas Woodrow Wilson was born in Staunton, Virginia, on December 28, 1856, the third child of Presbyterian minister Joseph Wilson and his wife, Jessie Woodrow Wilson. The Wilsons had moved to Virginia from Ohio, where Joseph and Jessie had been raised, and fully embraced southern life in the era leading up to the Civil War. The family lived in a three-story Greek Revival manse overlooking the town and were served by three enslaved staff, leased by the Presbyterian Church from a local farmer. In 1858, Reverend Wilson was offered a new job, and the family moved farther south to Augusta, Georgia, where they lived through the Civil War and most of Reconstruction. During the Civil War, Reverend Wilson served as a chaplain for the Confederate army and led a southern branch of the Presbyterian Church that argued in favor of slavery.

Tommy, as he was known to his family, struggled with reading and writing as a child, reportedly not learning to read fluently until he was ten years old. Despite this, his parents recognized that he was bright and spent a lot of time helping him with his studies. Tommy would later describe his father as his greatest teacher. As a teenager, Tommy took a correspondence course in which he learned shorthand, a skill he used throughout his career.

Tommy was taught at home and by tutors until he entered college—first a brief stint at Davidson College in North Carolina and then a time at the College of New Jersey (later renamed Princeton University). He began law school at the University of Virginia and practiced law for a short period. But he quickly decided he was more interested in the academic life and returned to school. He earned a PhD in political science from Johns Hopkins University in Maryland, making him the only U.S. president with an earned PhD.

An Academic Life

Thomas Woodrow Wilson met his first wife, Ellen Louise Axson, while visiting family in Georgia. Ellen was also the child of a Presbyterian minister and was a talented artist, largely painting impressionist-style landscapes. They married in 1885, as Wilson was finishing his graduate studies. They had three daughters, Margaret, Jessie and Eleanor. Ellen gave up much of her artistic pursuits to focus on homemaking and supporting her husband as he climbed the ranks in academia and then politics.

Wilson began his academic career as an instructor at Bryn Mawr College in Pennsylvania and Wesleyan University in Connecticut before getting a position at his alma mater, Princeton University. He was a popular teacher and rose quickly through the ranks, becoming president of Princeton University in 1902. By most reports, the Wilsons' years in Princeton were happy ones; Ellen raised the children and entertained university guests, and Woodrow (as he was by then known) was immersed in his research, writing and university life. Wilson authored a total of nine books on history and politics over the course of his career.

During his time at Princeton, Wilson caught the attention of New Jersey Democratic Party leaders who were looking for a candidate to run for New Jersey governor in 1910. They thought that Wilson's academic reputation

Woodrow and Ellen Wilson with their three daughters, Margaret, Eleanor and Jessie, circa 1912. *Library of Congress, Prints and Photographs Division.*

would benefit the Democratic Party but that his lack of political experience would make him easy to influence. Wilson won the election and then championed several bills that would limit the same political machine that got him into office. He also got several laws passed that improved working conditions for women, children and laborers, earning him the reputation as a "progressive" leader. Wilson served just one term as governor before setting his sights on the highest office in the land.

Our Twenty-Eighth President

Woodrow Wilson was the Democratic nominee for president in 1912, running against Republican William Howard Taft and former U.S. president Theodore Roosevelt, who campaigned under the newly formed Progressive Party. Thomas Marshall, the governor of Indiana, was Wilson's running mate. The Wilson-Marshall ticket garnered just 42 percent of the popular vote but an overwhelming majority of the electoral college vote. Wilson was sworn into office as the twenty-eighth president of the United States on March 4, 1913.

Historical reenactor Betsy Ely portraying Edith Bolling Wilson at the Edith Bolling Wilson Birthplace Museum. *Author's photograph*.

Wilson entered office with a progressive agenda and plans to crack down on the wealthy corporations and bankers that he and other Progressives believed were corrupting America's fair-market democracy. Highlights of Wilson's first term in office included the passage of laws that benefited small business owners by lowering tariffs (the Underwood Act), providing them easier access to loans (the Federal Reserve System) and creating a system to investigate and prosecute unfair business practices (the Federal Trade Commission). He also improved the lives of day laborers, creating laws against child labor and restricting railroad workers to an eight-hour workday. Wilson also instituted the first graduated federal income tax in 1913 with the Sixteenth Amendment, shifting the source of the bulk of federal funding from tariffs to taxes.

Despite these accomplishments, Wilson had a poor track record when it came to issues of racial equality. At Princeton, he discouraged Black students from enrolling. Wilson's book *A History of the American People* is sympathetic to the Ku Klux Klan. During his presidency, he resegregated several federal executive departments, escalated segregation in the armed forces and replaced Black ambassadors. By the standards of both today and the early twentieth century, Wilson enacted racist policies that set Black Americans back generations.

During his first term in office, Wilson lost his beloved wife Ellen. She suffered from kidney disease, succumbing in 1914. By all reports, Wilson was bereft; friends expressed concern that he was at a loss without female accompaniment. The following year, he was set up with the widow of a local businessman, Edith Bolling Galt, and they were married in December 1915.

The Great War and League of Nations

By the time of his 1916 reelection campaign, Wilson had shifted his focus to the Great War in Europe, which was, by then, well into its second year. Wilson ran against Republican and supreme court justice Charles Evans Hughes on a platform of neutrality: he promised to keep the United States out of the war in Europe. Wilson won the election by a closer margin than he had in 1913, but he would soon have to go back on his campaign promises.

In early 1917, German submarines began attacking U.S. merchant ships, and U.S. intelligence intercepted communications that suggested the

Woodrow Wilson seated at a desk, with his wife, Edith Bolling Wilson, standing at his side, 1920. This carefully posed photograph was released by the Wilsons to counter claims that Wilson had been incapacitated by his recent stroke. *Library of Congress, Prints and Photographs Division.*

Germans were trying to get Mexico to turn against the United States. Wilson could no longer keep the United States out of international affairs, and on April 2, 1917, he asked Congress to declare war against Germany. With American intervention, the war was brought to an end the following year, although not before more than one hundred thousand American soldiers were killed and twice that number were wounded.

Even prior to the armistice on November 11, 1918, Wilson began speaking publicly about his belief in the importance of international cooperation to ensure there would not be another great war in Europe or elsewhere. He advocated for what he called his Fourteen Points, which included redrawing national boundaries along ethnic lines, providing basic human rights protections to colonized nations and, most importantly, the establishment of an international peace-making organization: a League of Nations. Wilson spent months in Europe advocating for the formation of a League of Nations during the negotiations leading up to the Treaty of Versailles, but the Allied nations insisted on the economic and political punishment of Germany. This decision would eventually lead to a second war less than two decades later.

While negotiating peace in Europe, Wilson largely neglected the home front. He returned from the Paris Peace Conference in mid-1919 to discover that the political climate had shifted back home. Republicans had taken power during the midterm elections and were not supportive of Wilson's League of Nations, arguing that it could force the United States to become involved in more foreign wars. Wilson embarked on a speaking tour across the United States to advocate for his plan, hoping to persuade the public directly. He was a persuasive speaker but exhausted himself on the tour and had to cut it short. In October 1919, Wilson suffered a debilitating stroke, which paralyzed his left side and left him with only partial vision.

In 1919, there was no formal mechanism to replace an incapacitated president. Not until 1965 did Congress pass the Twenty-Fifth Amendment, which established the presidential chain of succession. When Wilson's stroke left him bedridden and cognitively compromised, his doctor and wife Edith decided to keep the severity of his condition secret from the public, the press, Congress and even Wilson's own cabinet.

For the next several months, Edith ran interference between her husband and the outside world. She would bring him correspondence, write his responses (allegedly from his dictations) and would not allow anyone other than his doctor and immediate family into his bedroom. When criticism reached the level that they felt they needed to respond, Edith staged a photoshoot with a still-paralyzed Wilson sitting at a desk, appearing to sign a document while she looks over his shoulder. By October 1920, Wilson had recovered enough to appear in public, but he never fully recovered and accomplished little during his last eighteen months in office.

The President Woodrow Wilson House in Washington, D.C. *Library of Congress, Prints and Photographs Division.*

The League of Nations proceeded in Europe without the United States' involvement; it would continue until the beginning of World War II and serve as a model for the future United Nations. Wilson received the 1919 Nobel Peace Prize for his role in creating the League of Nations, although it was likely bittersweet.

Retirement

Wilson served out the rest of his presidential term fairly quietly. After leaving the White House in 1921, the Wilsons moved into a house in Washington, D.C. Wilson's health never fully recovered, and he died just three years later on February 3, 1924. He was buried in the Washington National Cathedral in Washington, D.C.

WOODROW WILSON HISTORIC SITES IN VIRGINIA

WOODROW WILSON PRESIDENTIAL LIBRARY AND MUSEUM

20 North Coalter Street, Staunton, VA
(540) 885-0897
woodrowwilson.org

Woodrow Wilson was born in a Presbyterian manse in Staunton, Virginia, and lived there for the first seventeen months of his life. Although he only lived in Staunton for a short time, he considered it to be his hometown and returned many times over the course of his childhood and young adulthood to visit members of his extended family. After his death, Wilson's second wife, Edith Bolling Wilson, advocated and raised funds for the purchase and restoration of the manse as a shrine to her husband. The house was first opened for tours in 1941.

Wilson's birthplace is now part of the Woodrow Wilson Presidential Library and Museum. The museum's campus comprises the Woodrow Wilson Presidential Library, the Woodrow Wilson Museum, the presidential birthplace and a gift store. There are also terraced gardens with a walking path connecting the buildings.

The Woodrow Wilson Museum, located in a renovated historic home, includes exhibits about Wilson's life and times. Highlights include a re-creation of a World War I trench and the still-operational 1919 Pierce-Arrow limousine that was part of the presidential fleet and purchased by friends of Wilson after he left office. The museum is self-guided and open daily.

The presidential birthplace is a three-story Greek Revival Presbyterian manse—or minister's home—interpreted to the 1855–58 period during which the Wilson family lived there. The manse contains several artifacts connected to the family, including a crib and rocker that were used by the Wilson children and an early nineteenth-century clock that was given to the

An exhibit at the Woodrow Wilson Museum. *Courtesy of the Woodrow Wilson Presidential Library and Museum.*

family by the doctor who delivered Woodrow Wilson. The manse is open for guided tours daily.

The Woodrow Wilson Presidential Library contains books, photographs and archival material related to Woodrow Wilson, his family and the presidential birthplace. The presidential library is open by advance appointment only, although many of the photographs have been digitized and are available on the museum's website. (Wilson's presidential papers are held by the Library of Congress in Washington, D.C.)

The Woodrow Wilson Presidential Library and Museum offers thematic tours on occasion, including those focusing on the enslaved residents of the home and Victorian mourning traditions.

EDITH BOLLING WILSON BIRTHPLACE MUSEUM

145 East Main Street, Wytheville, VA
(276) 223-3484
edithbollingwilson.org

Woodrow Wilson's second wife, Edith Bolling, was born and raised in the small, rural town of Wytheville in the southwest corner of Virginia. The

The Edith Bolling Wilson Birthplace Museum, the childhood home of Wilson's second wife, in Wytheville. *Author's photograph.*

Bolling family home was located on the second floor of a brick commercial building in the center of town. The first floor of the building houses a small museum with artifacts and exhibits about Edith Bolling Wilson and guided tours are offered of the partially restored second floor. The museum is open by appointment, which can be made on the museum website.

Outside of Virginia

Boyhood Home of President Woodrow Wilson

419 Seventh Street, Augusta, GA
706-722-9828
wilsonboyhoodhome.org

The Wilsons left Staunton, Virginia, in 1858 for Reverend Wilson to take a position as minister of the First Presbyterian Church in Augusta, Georgia. Two years later, the church purchased this house in downtown Augusta, and the Wilsons moved in. They lived in the house throughout the Civil War and Reconstruction, leaving in 1870. The house is currently owned by Historic Augusta Inc. and operated as a historic house museum with artifacts from the Wilson family and their time. The museum is open daily for guided tours.

The Museum of the Reconstruction Era at the Woodrow Wilson Family Home

1705 Hampton Street, Columbia, SC
803-252-1770 extension 23
historiccolumbia.org/woodrow-wilson-family-home

The house where Woodrow Wilson lived as a teenager is located not far from the University of South Carolina in Columbia. The house was built in 1871 and was the only house that Woodrow Wilson's parents ever owned. It is currently owned by Richland County and managed by Historic Columbia as the Museum of the Reconstruction Era, with exhibits focusing on the post–Civil War period in Columbia and beyond. The museum is open daily.

PRESIDENT WOODROW WILSON HOUSE

2340 South Street, Washington, D.C.
202-387-4062
woodrowwilsonhouse.org

This 1915 Georgian Revival townhouse was purchased by Woodrow Wilson and his second wife, Edith, after they left the White House in 1921. Woodrow lived out the last three years of his life in the home, and Edith remained in the house until her death in 1961. Upon her death, Edith left the house and many of its contents to the National Trust for Historic Preservation, which has operated it as a historic house museum since 1963.

The house contains many of the Wilsons' personal belongings, including furniture, clothing and books. The drawing room features a selection of fine art and souvenirs given to Wilson by dignitaries from around the world. (During Wilson's era, presidents were permitted to keep such gifts when they left office; this is no longer the case.) In addition to the Wilsons' bedrooms, dining room and library, the house tour includes spaces that

The library in the President Woodrow Wilson House in Washington, D.C. *Courtesy of the President Woodrow Wilson House.*

were used by the Wilsons' staff: a nurse's room, butler's pantry and circa-1920s kitchen.

The President Woodrow Wilson House is located in the Kalorama neighborhood of Washington, D.C., near many of the foreign embassies and just off Dupont Circle. The house is open daily for guided tours.

WASHINGTON NATIONAL CATHEDRAL

3101 Wisconsin Avenue Northwest, Washington, D.C.
202-537-6200
cathedral.org

Woodrow Wilson died on February 3, 1924, and was buried in the Washington National Cathedral. The cathedral is open daily for self-guided tours if there is not a special event scheduled. His tomb is located to the right after one enters the cathedral.

9

OTHER PRESIDENTIAL SITES
IN VIRGINIA

I n addition to the Virginia-born presidents, four other U.S. presidents have connections to the Old Dominion; two were buried here and two others had summer homes in the Virginia mountains.

WILLIAM HOWARD TAFT

William Howard Taft (1857–1930), the twenty-seventh president of the United States, was born in Ohio, graduated from Yale University and then went on to study law. He worked as a judge, the governor of the Philippines and secretary of war under President Theodore Roosevelt before obtaining the highest seat in the land in 1908. Taft led the nation from 1909 to 1913 and is best known for stalling the progressive momentum of his predecessor and mentor Theodore Roosevelt. Taft lost to Woodrow Wilson in the 1912 presidential election and later served as chief justice on the supreme court—a position that he apparently greatly preferred to being president— until shortly before his death from heart disease. His widow selected the site where Taft was buried in what was then an undeveloped section of Arlington National Cemetery. His headstone was designed by American sculptor James Earle Fraser, who also designed the National Archives and supreme court buildings in Washington, D.C. His widow, Helen Herron Taft (1861–1943), was also interred there; she is best known for arranging the planting of more than three thousand cherry trees near the Jefferson Memorial in Washington, D.C., in 1912.

JOHN F. KENNEDY

John F. Kennedy (1917–1963), the thirty-fifth president of the United States, was a born-and-bred New Englander, and his presidential library/museum is a masterpiece located on the Columbia Point waterfront in Boston, Massachusetts. Kennedy attended Harvard then joined the U.S. Navy and served in the Pacific theater during World War II. Kennedy served more than a decade in Congress before winning an election to the White House in 1960, making him the first Catholic and youngest president elected to office. After Kennedy's 1963 assassination in Dallas, Texas, his widow wanted him buried somewhere that was accessible to the American public. Jackie Kennedy selected a site on a hill in Arlington National Cemetery, overlooking the Lincoln Memorial and surrounded by a white picket fence. However, the site was swamped with so many visitors that officials determined a more suitable location was needed to manage the crowds. In 1967, Kennedy was reinterred at his grave's present location, which includes a walkway, a granite observation area and an eternal flame. Jacqueline Lee Kennedy Onassis (1929–1994) and two of the Kennedys' children who died in infancy were also interred there.

ARLINGTON NATIONAL CEMETERY
Arlington, VA
877-907-8585
arlingtoncemetery.mil

In addition to the two presidents buried here, Arlington National Cemetery has a connection to the nation's first president. Arlington House, an 1818 Greek Revival mansion that overlooks the cemetery, was originally built as a memorial to George Washington by his step-grandson. The land that now comprises Arlington National Cemetery once belonged to George Washington's stepson, John "Jack" Parke Custis. His son, George Washington Parke Custis, inherited the 1,100-acre plantation in 1802 and built a mansion to serve as his home and to display his Washington memorabilia. George Custis's daughter, Mary Anna Randolph Custis, became the second wife of Robert E. Lee, who led the Confederate army during the Civil War. (Lee's first wife was the daughter of Zachary Taylor.) The Lees inherited the estate and the ownership of its 196 enslaved laborers in 1857 and lived there until the outbreak of the Civil War. The

John F. Kennedy's grave site at Arlington National Cemetery, with Arlington House in the background. *Arlington National Cemetery*.

land was confiscated by the U.S. government for the Lees' failure to pay taxes and served as an army camp and planned community for freed Black people. The land was eventually incorporated as a burial ground for U.S. service members and their families in 1900. Arlington House is currently operated by the National Park Service as a memorial to Robert E. Lee, with exhibits about the history of the house, the enslaved people who lived on the plantation and Lee.

Arlington National Cemetery is open daily.

THEODORE ROOSEVELT

Theodore Roosevelt Jr. (1858–1919) was born and raised in New York City but championed outdoor life. Among Roosevelt's accomplishments during his presidency from 1901 to 1909 was the preservation of land in the western United States, where he also owned land.

PINE KNOT
Keene, VA
434-286-6106
pineknot.org

In 1905, Edith Roosevelt purchased fifteen acres and a rustic cabin in Albemarle County to serve as a retreat for herself and her husband, the twenty-sixth president of the United States, Theodore Roosevelt.

Pine Knot is now owned by a volunteer nonprofit organization and is open for tours by appointment, available on its website.

HERBERT HOOVER

The thirty-first president of the United States is best known for navigating the nation through the depths of the Great Depression. Herbert Hoover (1874–1964) served one term in office, from 1929 to 1933.

RAPIDAN CAMP
Shenandoah National Park, VA
540-999-3500
nps.gov/thingstodo/rapidan-camp.htm

In 1929, Herbert Hoover purchased 164 acres of land in the Blue Ridge Mountains of western Virginia to serve as a summer White House during his presidency. The U.S. Marine Corps built thirteen buildings at the site, including meeting spaces, dormitories and a Brown House for the president. All were connected by paths that were designed to blend in with their surroundings and provide a serene retreat and workspace for the thirty-first president, his family and colleagues.

The Hoovers donated Rapidan Camp to the Commonwealth of Virginia, and it became a part of Shenandoah National Park in 1935. It was deemed too remote to be used by subsequent presidents, although some did visit the site. All but three of the camp's buildings were torn down in 1959.

Rapidan Camp is now accessible via a four-mile (round trip) hike from the Milam Gap parking area at mile 52 on Skyline Drive in Shenandoah National Park. The Brown House has been restored to its 1932 appearance, and an adjoining cabin contains an exhibit about the history of the camp. Both are open to ranger-led tours during the summer.

BIBLIOGRAPHY

Appleby, Joyce Oldham. *Thomas Jefferson*. New York: Holt, 2003.

Bachman, Walt. *The Last White House Slaves: The Story of Jane, President Zachary Taylor's Enslaved Concubine*. Independently published, 2019.

Bernstein, Richard B. *Thomas Jefferson*. New York: Oxford University Press, 2003.

Cheney, Lynne. *James Madison: A Life Reconsidered*. New York: Viking, 2014.

Coe, Alexis. *You Never Forget Your First: A Biography of George Washington*. New York: Viking, 2020.

Collins, Gail. *William Henry Harrison*. New York: Times Books, 2012.

Cooper, John Milton, Jr. *Woodrow Wilson: A Biography*. New York: Vintage Books, 2011.

Crapol, Edward P. *John Tyler: The Accidental President*. Chapel Hill: University of North Carolina Press, 2013.

Eisenhower, John S.D. *Zachary Taylor*. New York: Times Books, 2008.

Ellis, Joseph J. *His Excellency: George Washington*. New York: Vintage Books, 2004.

Gordon-Reed, Annette. *The Hemingses of Monticello: An American Family*. New York: W.W. Norton and Co., 2009.

Hamilton, Holman. *Zachary Taylor: Soldier of the Republic*. Indianapolis: Bobbs-Merrill, 1941.

Hamilton, Neil A., and Ian C. Friedman. *Presidents: A Biographical Dictionary*. New York: Facts on File, 2010.

Hart, Gary. *James Monroe*. New York: Times Books, 2012.

Janken, Kenneth Robert. *Walter White: Mr. NAACP*. Chapel Hill: University of North Carolina Press, 2006.

Kearse, Bettye. *The Other Madisons: The Lost History of a President's Black Family*. New York: Houghton Mifflin Harcourt, 2020.

Leahy, Christopher J. *President Without a Party: The Life of John Tyler*. Baton Rouge: Louisiana State University Press, 2020.

Maass, John R. *George Washington's Virginia*. Charleston, SC: The History Press, 2017.

Macaluso, Laura A. *A Guide to Thomas Jefferson's Virginia*. Charleston, SC: The History Press, 2018.

Miller, Charley, and Peter Miller. *Monticello: The Official Guide to Thomas Jefferson's World*. Washington, D.C.: National Geographic, 2016.

Miller, Kristie. *Ellen and Edith: Woodrow Wilson's First Ladies*. Lawrence: University Press of Kansas, 2015.

Walker, Jane C. *John Tyler: A President of Many Firsts*. Blacksburg, VA: McDonald and Woodward, 2001.

Wills, Garry. *James Madison*. New York: Times Books, 2002.

Children's Books

Bains, Rae, and Hal Frenck. *James Monroe: Young Patriot*. Mahwah, NJ: Troll Associates, 1986.

Bauer, K. Jack. *Zachary Taylor: Soldier, Planter, Statesman of the Old West*. Baton Rouge: Louisiana State University Press, 1985.

Brunelli, Carol. *Zachary Taylor: Our 12th President*. Mankato, MN: Child's World, 2021.

Brunelli, Carol, and Ann Gaines. *Woodrow Wilson: Our 28th President*. Mankato, MN: Child's World, 2021.

Ferry, Steven. *John Tyler: Our 10th President*. Mankato, MN: Child's World, 2021.

Fritz, Jean. *The Great Little Madison*. New York: Puffin Books, 2014.

Gaines, Ann. *George Washington: Our 1st President*. Mankato, MN: Child's World, 2021.

———. *James Madison: Our 4th President*. Mankato, MN: Child's World, 2021.

———. *James Monroe: Our 5th President*. Mankato, MN: Child's World, 2021.

———. *William Henry Harrison: Our 9th President*. Mankato, MN: Child's World, 2021.

Mitchell, Barbara, and Alex Tavoularis. *Father of the Constitution: A Story About James Madison*. Minneapolis: Carolrhoda Books, 2004.

Peckham, Howard Henry, and Patrick H. Lawlor. *William Henry Harrison: Young Tippecanoe*. Solon, OH: Findaway World, 2007.

Sirimarco, Elizabeth. *Thomas Jefferson: Our 3rd President*. Mankato, MN: Child's World, 2021.

Websites

Digital Montpelier Project. www.digitalmontpelier.org.

Miller Center, University of Virginia. www.millercenter.org.

President John Tyler's Enslaved Households. www.presidentjohntylersenslavedhouseholds.com.

Take Them in Families. www.taketheminfamilies.com.

White House Historical Association. www.whitehousehistory.org.

INDEX

ABOUT THE AUTHOR

H eather S. Cole is a writer and public historian living in the Shenandoah Valley of Virginia. She has worked in a variety of museums and archives, including as an interpreter at the Woodrow Wilson Presidential Library and Museum in Staunton, Virginia. This is her third book for The History Press.